No Grid Survival Projects •

[12 Books in 1]

The Ultimate DIY Guide for Self-Sufficiency.Master Tested Projects to Survive Crisis and Recession.2000 Days of Ingenious Ideas for Self-Reliance

Anthony Jensen

done without written consent and can in no way be considered an endorsement from the trademark holder

Contents

INTRODUCTION

In the current world we live in now, we depend on the power grid for most of our daily needs. Our homes, companies, and technology are all run by electricity. This may seem like a comfort, but it also makes us subject to power cuts, natural disasters, and other situations. Because of this, a lot of people are looking to off-grid life and survival projects that don't depend on the power grid. In this book, we'll look at the Bible and talk about no grid survival projects. The Bible has a lot of information and advice about how to live off the land and be independent. We will look at the different lessons and concepts from the Bible that can be used in current off-grid life. From how to grow your own food to how to build your own home, the Bible has a lot to teach you about how to live off the land and survive without electricity.

In this book, we'll look at all the ways the Bible can be used as a complete guide for off-grid survival projects. We will look more closely at the Bible's practical advice, such as how to grow a yard, raise animals, and store food, as well as the spiritual and moral values that support a self-sufficient way of life.

Book 1: The Art of Self-Reliance: Mastering the Skills for a Self-Sufficient Life

World fragility has never been higher. We face various threats, including nuclear war. Some individuals live off-grid to prepare for anything due to this vulnerability. What is off-grid living? How to get it? Is self-sufficiency feasible without land? This chapter discusses self-sufficiency and why survivalists and preppers need it!

Survival skills

Self-sufficiency starts with survival skills. Find food, water, shelter, and avoid predators.

Learn these essential survival skills immediately! Many internet tools can teach you these abilities without leaving your sofa.

Off-grid homes

Build shelter and comfort to live off-grid. It's crucial to know which structure is ideal for your scenario.

Generating power

Solar panels are useful for self-generation. They charge batteries and power devices. They may be used with wind turbines and other alternative energy sources for improved efficiency. They can't generate power if it's overcast or rainy.

Culinary possibilities

Fire grills meat, fish, and vegetables. Solar ovens prepare food.

Grilling: A campfire or fire pit is all you need to cook. It cooks steaks, burgers, and chicken breasts seasoned in your chosen flavors.

Solar ovens are fantastic for baking breads, cakes, and cookies when you don't have power or gas!

Water sanitation solutions

Bathrooms are crucial to your house. You shower, brush your teeth, wash your hands and face, and get ready for bed here. What if there's no flowing water? How can you clean without it?

An outdoor shower is useful for washing off dirt before entering the home. If space or privacy issues prevent this, everyone must learn how to utilize sand as a personal exfoliator! Sanding down after a day hunting or fishing can eradicate any germs or bacteria that may have developed on our body. Who doesn't enjoy getting down with nature?

Self-sufficient living

Community gardens are fantastic places to start gardening and growing food. They're also a terrific chance to meet other sustainability enthusiasts.

Join a homesteading or off-grid lifestyle forum. Many of these sites have active forums where people discuss gardening, livestock care, constructing homes without power tools, cooking without electricity or gas stoves, and more!

Get water.

Water matters most. First and foremost, you need clean water to survive. Water is fantastic! If you're off-grid and drinking rainfall or stream water, be sure it's safe. Untreated, this might cause disease or death.

Purify water.

Water purification is a crucial survival skill. As you know, polluted water may cause many diseases and death. These actions will ensure your drinking water is safe:

Boil water over an open fire or electric cooktop burner (if available) to purify it.

If boiling isn't possible, use iodine tablets or bleach to purify, but check with local authorities first because some areas have laws against using iodine for purification due to its health risks, especially when misused!

Plan sanitation.

Survival requires sanitation. When you're focused on survival, it's tempting to disregard cleanliness, yet doing so greatly increases your risk of illness.

Hand washing and bathing need adequate water. If you don't have flowing water, store it in huge plastic tubs.

Dig a 6-8-inch hole outside the perimeter fence or wall line at least 200 feet from any facility where people sleep or assemble to teach everyone how to properly dispose of human waste. Use toilet paper sparingly and bury it with feces; do not burn it since the ashes may contain diseases that might pollute groundwater!

Find emergency care.

This is crucial to preparation. If you or a neighbor needs medical care, you should know where to go. Due to power and infrastructural shortages, many hospitals and clinics will be closed. Many hospitals can't cure patients without electricity!

Find out which hospitals have generators. whether this information isn't online or doesn't seem promising, phone the hospital and ask what their emergency power strategy is or whether they have backup power sources! Ask about their surgical and critical care capabilities.

Plan for self-sufficiency.

Building a self-sufficient farm or off-grid cottage requires forethought.

Learn about your food-growing and animal-raising possibilities. You must also learn how to catch rainwater and store it in barrels or cisterns for year-round usage.

Earthbag dome houses are cheaper and easier to construct than log cottages, which need more expertise and cost more.

Independence means self-sufficiency.

It's about supporting yourself and others without help. It's also about surviving emergency or everyday situations.

We use phones for everything from calling friends and family to ordering meals from restaurants when we're too busy or lazy to prepare! What if the electricity fails? No cell services? How will individuals acquire self-care information?

Several techniques may attain self-sufficiency.

Self-sufficiency is a shared goal. We will cover some of the various methods to do so.

Solar power allows electrical self-sufficiency. Solar power uses the sun's energy throughout the day and stores it in batteries for nighttime or cloudy days. If you reside in Arizona, you may install solar panels on your roof. Before buying or installing any solar panels, be sure they'll work for your home's location.

Self-sufficiency may be achieved step-by-step.

Self-sufficiency begins with food production. Starting a garden or growing hens and bees can achieve this, but it's hard. It may take some trial and error to find the finest plants for your location and how much space they require. "In addition, if the soil in your yard isn't already rich in nutrients (or if it contains harmful chemicals), planting anything could be difficult without adding compost or fertilizer first--and even then, certain plants may not thrive without extra care from an expert gardener who knows exactly what kind of dirt needs what kind of nutrients added back into it over time before being planted again next year."

Self-sufficiency starts with food, water, shelter, and clothing, and then you can move on to community building and gardening.

- Grow your own food to become self-sufficient.
- Self-sufficiency requires skills and mindset.
- You can overcome anything with the proper mindset.

This book will teach you how modern civilization works and why it might fail under certain conditions. If we want to live with less dependence on external systems like electricity grids, we need to understand how they work in the first place.

Self-sufficiency means providing for oneself.

Self-sufficiency is an essential notion in many cultures, but it was notably stressed during the 1960s and 1970s back-to-land movement.

Self-sufficiency is being able to provide for oneself on your own property, including food and shelter.

Providing life's needs

- Preppers and survivalists should learn how to live off the land for several reasons, including saving money in terrible times.

- We can only protect ourselves from rising costs by taking steps now to become self-sufficient in the event of a disaster or economic collapse.
- You may be wondering what it means to be self-sufficient. In our modern world, that usually means being able to grow a variety of crops and raise animals for food, building shelter, heat, and power generation. If you want to live off-grid in a rural setting, you will probably need to become more self-reliant than most grid-connected property owners, especially if they live near supermarkets!

This chapter will teach you how to cultivate organic vegetables and fruit without land or water, even if you live in a developed nation.

Most individuals don't know how to raise their own food without pesticides or herbicides.

No-Grid Survival Projects is here to educate you how to cultivate your own organic food, even in an urban area with limited space and resources.

Self-sufficiency is not about cultivating enormous fields of maize, wheat, or soybeans (although these are essential), but about making the most of what you have, turning waste into useable resources, and utilizing nature as much as possible to avoid needing man-made items.

If you want to go completely off the grid, you'll need a way to generate electricity and heat your home without using fossil fuels like coal or oil. Solar panels can generate electricity, but if there's no sun where you live, they won't work well unless they're paired with other power generation methods like wind turbines, which use an alternator to convert kinetic energy into mechanical work.

This guide is for those who want only minimal self-sufficiency while still living within society's norms, so I won't go into detail about how these systems work, but suffice it to say that they do exist!

Vegetables grow easily.
This course will teach you the fundamentals of growing veggies and herbs.

Self-sufficiency in gardening means that you have everything you need to survive without outside help or intervention (i.e., no grid). If something goes wrong with your garden, like a drought or insect infestation, you're the only one who can save it. That's why growing vegetables is an important part of any no-grid survival project or homesteading project.

Grow and construct what you can.
- Learn what you can cultivate and construct to become self-sufficient.
- Before planting, you should know what plants and trees are natural to your location, how much room you have, and how much time you want to spend in the yard.
- Grow vegetables in old tires, buckets, pots, etc.
- Greenhouse your garden beds with a tarp or sheet.
- Plant seeds that are resilient in colder climes and seasonal for your location (e.g., lettuce and spinach grow best in spring and autumn).

Build a greenhouse for early planting.
- If you want tomatoes to be ready for harvest by mid-summer, you can start them in February under lights in the greenhouse and transplant them out in May.
- Grow black soldier fly larvae to decompose kitchen trash.
- Black soldier flies are a great source of protein and fat, but they only eat organic matter. If you raise chickens or ducks, you can feed the larvae their manure, or you can use kitchen scraps, garden trimmings, or weeds.
- With a proper enclosure (see our DIY bug hotels page), black soldier flies may be raised inside, but we prefer keeping them outdoors where their natural predators won't disturb them.

Learn worm composting and acquire them.
Worms are fantastic pets and composters.

Worms are simple to maintain and don't take up much room. You may purchase them online, at a pet shop, or from friends, but make sure they're compatible for your environment (wood-eating worms won't survive in hot climes).

If you're new to keeping hens, start with one or two from a local farmer. After a few months, try growing your flock!

Some breeds are good mothers, while others aren't and might need more attention from the owner if they want chicks every year. A chicken's breed can also affect how much meat it produces when slaughtered, so keep this in mind when choosing a breed.

A solar oven can cook meals for extended periods without fuel or power.

First, make an insulated cardboard or wood box with a secure lid:

- This design works well since it permits air circulation and insulation from heat loss during usage, but it also keeps wind and rain from entering your solar oven while it's not in use.
- Now you need to reflect light onto your food, which is called passive radiation heating because no electricity is used. You can use aluminum foil or even tin foil, but make sure it doesn't absorb too much heat before placing it on our cardboard box frame.
- Build a solar still to gather water from plants that don't require groundwater or rains.
- A solar still uses heat and evaporation to collect plant moisture and condense it into drinkable water. It works in an enclosed, clear plastic bag that lets sunlight pass through it, making the air inside hot and humid and forming condensation on both sides of the bag (one side being cooler than the other).

Producing your own food and other necessities reduces the energy needed to transport them from producers to consumers, which reduces air pollution, greenhouse gas emissions, and other negative effects of fossil fuels.

There are many ways to become self-sufficient, but it all comes down to attitude and hard work. It may take time, but your skills will improve until they become second nature!

Book 2: How to Grow Vegetable Garden

Even without power, gardening is a great method to sustain oneself. Growing your own food requires the correct equipment. Your survival garden's location is crucial.

Vegetable Garden Plants

- Potatoes
- Carrots
- Beets
- Radishes
- Salad greens—lettuce

Vegetable Garden Benefits

- Vegetable gardens offer fresh, healthful food year-round. It provides food and more:
- outdoor recreation
- An opportunity to exercise through gardening or wandering about it
- Emergency self-reliance

Survival Gardening

- Growing veggies helps you prepare for emergencies.
- Even with limited room and time, growing your own veggies is simple.
- Plant veggies in containers, raised beds, or the ground.
- Survival Garden Site Selection
- Start your survival garden in a bright site with at least six hours of sunshine. Consider soil quality, drainage, and impediments to vegetable growth.
- If you have the room, build raised beds with topsoil and compost or manure. If you want something fast and simple, create or purchase them online. If not, drill holes for each plant—just make sure they're deep enough to avoid disturbing roots while refilling!

These ideas can help you harvest enough of veggies this year.
- Climate-appropriate veggies.
- Plant pots, raised beds, or gardens.
- Mulch keeps weeds down and soil wet.
- Deeply water weekly or less.

- Fresh veggies all summer!
- Grid-tied vs. no-grid systems.

No-grid has various benefits. First, you don't need grid electricity or water. This technique may be utilized during outages or while going off-grid. Because it employs solar panels and batteries instead of an electric company producing energy from its grid system and sending bills each month, it saves money on both fronts: no electric company payments, no costly batteries or power generators!

No more brownouts or blackouts! If there's another hurricane like Hurricane Sandy, which caused blackouts in New York City in 2012, "you won't lose any valuable food because everything will still be stored safely inside refrigerators where they won't spoil until they're needed again later down the road once things get back up running smoothly."

Solar panels and a controller manage the electricity they create so they don't overload or undercharge the batteries, which store the energy and power lights and other appliances.

This may be done in any size garden, but start small with one or two plants. Once you're comfortable producing your own food and have mastered gardening, you can add additional plants.

Successful gardening requires
A thriving garden requires adequate sunshine, food, water, and air for all veggies.

If you live in an area with little sun or frequent cloud cover, consider planting lettuce or other low-light crops.

In warm weather, your plants will grow quicker than you expect. With proper water and sunshine, your vegetable garden can feed your family.

Till your garden till planting.
Tilling and adding compost or fertilizer before planting can help your plants grow robust and healthy.

If you don't have a shovel, you may till your garden bed without one:

Use a hoe (a long-handled implement with an angled blade) to scrape the ground and rake away any weeds.

Hand tilling involves digging up and discarding pieces of dirt.

Plants suffer in winter everywhere.

- If you're growing vegetables in northern climates where temperatures regularly drop below freezing (32 degrees F), here's what you need to know: Most garden plants go dormant in winter, stopping growth and storing nutrients in their roots.
- For winter moisture retention, cover your soil with at least 6 inches of compost or manure before planting.
- Kale and cabbage, developed for cold environments, can stay longer without frostbite protection than tomatoes and peppers.
- Transplant your indoor-started seedlings.
- If you're growing a garden for off-grid survival, start your seeds indoors so they can grow in their new environment before winter.

Grow in pots.
"But I want a vegetable garden!" How without a grid?"

You can grow vegetables in the ground using earth and water in any container, even an old bucket.

- Easy-to-harvest and store crops.
- Choose easy-to-harvest and store crops.
- Start a garden only if you have time and energy.
- Tomatoes and beans are simple to harvest and preserve.
- Diversify crops to prevent crop failure.
- Planting a variety of crops can help your garden succeed and feed your family.

If you're planting in raised beds, make sure they're at least 12 inches deep and wide enough to accommodate each plant's roots (the width should be twice as wide as the root ball). Avoid planting anything closer than 6 inches apart to improve air circulation around each plant's roots and encourage deeper root growth, which helps prevent drought stress in hot summers.

Companion plant.

Companion planting is a method used in agriculture to boost plant development by pairing helpful species.

- When the power goes down, nothing beats homegrown vegetables!
- How to develop veggies in a Small Space Growing veggies is a terrific way to get food on the table and learn about how plants develop and what they require.
- Survival garden location?
- The best place to grow a survival garden is in an area that gets plenty of sun. Vegetables need at least 6 hours of direct sunlight per day. If you live in an area with long periods without sunlight (winter), choose plants that will tolerate your climate and produce during these periods.
- If you plant your survival garden inside, make sure it gets enough of natural light and utilize artificial lighting until your plants are big enough to shade overhead lights or windowsills.

Survival gardens produce what vegetables?

Most veggies are simple to cultivate and will keep you healthy in a crisis, but others are harder.

- Potatoes: Hardy and easy to raise, potatoes may be stored for winter eating.
- Onions: Onions are another fantastic survival garden plant since you just need to water them infrequently and keep them out of direct sunlight.
- Tomatoes: Unlike potatoes and onions, tomatoes require warmer temperatures and lots of sun (or artificial light) to produce fruit, but if done right, they can produce an abundance of tasty fruits that last well into winter without refrigeration or freezing.

Making vegetable garden soil: how?

In this chapter, I'll show you how to make compost from household waste like leaves and other organic matter so you can start a vegetable garden in your backyard without a lot of space. Soil is one of the most important parts of gardening.

First, we need a place to put our compost pile, which can be made out of wood, metal, or cardboard (just make sure it's sturdy).

Which solar greenhouse tools are essential?
- Start with these essentials:
- Shovel and hoe
- A rake
- Garden or pitchfork

Survival gardens need how much sunlight?
If you reside in a region that doesn't receive much sunshine in winter or early spring, try putting artificial lights on your plants. Vegetables require at least six hours of direct sunlight every day.

Survival garden care.
Water your plants frequently, but don't overwater them—the roots will rot and the plant will die. Don't use water from ponds or rivers since it may contain toxic chemicals.

Without electricity
Keep it well-watered and give it enough sunshine to photosynthesize food. If you don't, your garden won't develop correctly or at all.

- Keep Your Garden Neat
- A neat garden helps you discover what you need and prevents bugs from damaging your veggies.
- Raised beds are easier to maintain and drain better. If you don't have room, create containers!
- Composting is vital to sustainable gardening!
- Mark Creatively
- Instead of squares or rectangles, employ diverse shapes and patterns to spice up a typical grid system.
- If you're ambitious and have time, consider circular gardens instead of squares for an organic look that will wow guests!

Use Pots and Containers for Indoor Vegetable Gardens.
Containers are a great way to grow vegetables if you have limited space. They can be placed on decks, patios, or even indoors on windowsills.

Kohlrabi, an easy-to-grow root crop, prefers a more alkaline pH and does not do well in soil fertilized with animal waste products like manure or chicken litter.

A vegetable garden has several uses than raising food for no grid survivalists:

It supplies fresh produce year-round (excluding winter) and reduces store dependence and food expenditures per serving by eliminating shipping and storage expenses.

Plan Next Year's Plants

Now that you know what to plant, it's time to start planning next year's garden. The best way to do this is by making a list of which plants did well and which ones didn't. You can also use this time to research new plants that might work in your climate or soil.

Vegetable garden planning.

Vegetables are essential to any homestead, but growing them in an urban location may be difficult. You may not have enough ground or soil, so you'll need to be inventive and use vertical space if feasible.

Planting seeds or seedlings in old pots lets you grow plants on balconies and patios that are too tiny.

Plant veggies on window boxes or balconies.

Choose wisely.

Before planting anything, you need to choose a spot with suitable soil.

- Next, consider sunlight: vegetables need at least six hours of direct sunlight per day to grow properly. If you live in an area with less direct sunlight, consider using fluorescent or LED grow lights instead of growing them outdoors.
- Replace earth beds with raised beds.
- If you have little room or bad soil, this is an excellent option to start a garden since it doesn't require much watering and can be protected from pests using mesh or netting.

- Raised beds don't become compacted by wind or water erosion, thus they need less care than earth beds.
- Use repurposed or cheap wall materials.
- Build your walls from old pallets, straw bales, bricks, or tires if you have a big yard!
- Add organic stuff if required.

If you don't have access to a lab, you can test your soil at home by taking a handful of dirt from different parts of your yard and adding water until it forms a ball that holds together but breaks apart easily when squeezed between two fingers (like Play-Doh).

- Plant your vegetables two weeks after the last frost.
- Check the USDA webpage for your region's final frost date to grow veggies.
- Due to the warm temperatures and lack of snow, you may be tempted to start planting earlier than this, but don't! Early spring weather can be unpredictable and inconsistent, which could cause your seedlings to get too much or too little water and die.

Water often.
Water periodically and weed with mulch, row coverings, or hand weeding until they are established and growing well.

You can also grow vegetables in containers on your balcony or patio. Most vegetables need at least six hours of sunlight a day, so choose a spot that gets at least that much. If you have more shade, try planting tomatoes in an old tire (or an inexpensive planter) and hanging it under a tree branch for dappled light.

Zero-grid vegetable garden
The first stage in developing a vegetable garden is choosing which veggies to produce, then choosing where to grow them, how much area they will take up, and what sort of soil or atmosphere they require.

- After that, you may sow seeds in your garden beds or start seedlings inside.
- Vegetable garden placement

- Vegetable gardens require sunshine, water, and nutrient-rich soil.
- If feasible, find a spot near windows in your house or apartment with plenty of natural light for your vegetable garden. If not, use LED lights.
- Next, choose the finest soil for various vegetables:

Grow plants from seedlings.
Start with seedlings and cultivate your own plants if you have seeds, or purchase them at the store if you don't.

Start with soil from a garden store, then acquire some little pots (like bathroom supply containers) to plant right away.

Choose the correct vegetable garden soil.
The most important thing about your soil is that it's fertile and healthy, with plenty of nutrients and minerals and loose enough for roots to grow. If your garden bed is too compacted or boggy, the vegetables won't get enough oxygen.

You can test your soil by taking a sample to your local agriculture office, which will tell you if there are any nutrient deficiencies (like iron). If they do, you can add fertilizer based on their recommendation, but don't overdo it! Too much fertilizer causes weeds and excess nitrogen in the plant, which turns its leaves yellow or brown before they die.

Vegetable garden watering.
Watering your vegetable garden is crucial to its health.

If you're growing vegetables in sandy or clayey loam, water them daily for 20 minutes at least once or twice a week during the hottest months of summer (July and August).

- Vegetable gardening.
- Avoid weeds.
- Water plants often.
- Pick your veggies when they're ready to avoid wasting them!
- Growing your own veggies is a terrific way to feed yourself and acquire gardening skills you can use elsewhere.

Here are some strategies for establishing a vegetable garden without power or gas

- There are many methods to raise your own food, even with a little area!
- Some people like raised beds, where they put boards or bricks on top of the ground to create little boxes for their plants. These are good because they keep water from getting into the soil and making it too wet for plants to grow well (although some people put gravel at the bottom to drain water). Others like growing vegetables in containers on their balconies.
- The first step in growing your own vegetables is choosing a spot that gets plenty of sunlight, has good drainage, and can be improved with compost or fertilizer. If you're planting in the ground, make sure there are no rocks or large roots (like tree stumps) underneath.
- Decide when to plant.
- Spring is the greatest season to grow a vegetable garden, usually March through June.
- If your garden doesn't receive enough sun, move it!
- Prioritize gardening.
- If you have limited room and finances for gardening, emphasize healthful and easy-to-store crops.
- Choose easy-to-grow crops like lettuce, spinach, and asparagus, which are worth the effort to plant and harvest.

Garden Watering and Fertilizing.

If you use rainwater, make sure it doesn't contain chemicals that could harm your plants. You can also use ponds or rivers, but they may be harder to access than a barrel or rainwater source.

Fertilizing Your Garden: Add composted leaves and other organic waste to your vegetable garden to nourish it and deter pests!

- Organically manage pests and illnesses.
- Companion planting attracts beneficial insects and repels pests.
- Food security is crucial and achievable!
- Food security and self-sufficiency are possible!

- With a little space and patience, you can raise all the veggies you need for yourself and your family.

If you found this chapter helpful, please share it with your friends and family who might be interested in growing their own food! Don't forget about those seeds—it's never too early or too late to start planning for next year's crops.

Book 3: How to Grow the Family Orchard

Growing fruit trees helps with food self-sufficiency. It provides you year-round fresh fruit and an orchard that can help you withstand a power outage.

Fruit orchard planting

Starting a fruit orchard begins with choosing a crop. Choose carefully from the various fruit tree varieties. Apple trees may not be the greatest option for your family if you live in a cold climate with snowfall. If you live in a place like mine, where temps are pleasant year-round, apples may grow nicely too!

You'll need room next! You need enough land so that all of your trees have room to grow without being crowded with other plants around them; otherwise, they might get sick or die because they don't have enough minerals coming up through their roots into their bodies anymore because everything else has used up all those nutrients currently by growing bigger than themselves before.

- Orcharding edible plants
- Plant trees.
- Plant shrubs.
- Plant vines.
- Survival-sized growth
- Grow enough apples for the entire family in a little area!

Here's how:

- Apple tree planting is simple but time-consuming. Plant them in your garden in April. If you don't have a garden, put your trees in a sunny spot—they'll grow without soil as long as they have something to hold onto.
- After winter, remove dead branches off your tree(s) to prevent weak places as it grows. This prevents bugs from invading later!
- Fruit trees and plants may flourish without grids.
- Fruit trees are great for growing food because:
- Offer wonderful fresh or preserved fruit.

- Need weekly watering once established.
- Fruit trees bear fruit for decades!

The fundamentals

Fruit tree growth may be learned quickly, but mastery requires more than reading books or watching YouTube videos. You must work hard.

Discover which trees fit your climate, soil, and location.

Use internet tools like this one from the USDA to help you pick types that thrive well in your location, and plant numerous varieties in case one fails due to weather or pests!

Climate matters.

Climate determines what to grow in every garden. Fruit trees in Arizona and New Mexico require additional water in summer. If you reside on the coast and get a lot of rain, pick drought-resistant peach, nectarine, or olive trees.

Prepare your kids.

Planning ahead with your kids helps meet everyone's demands and gets them engaged in the endeavor.

Consider how many trees you can grow when developing a family orchard. If it's too tiny, plant bushes so everyone can have their preferred fruit or nut tree.

Select healthy produce.

Choose healthy produce. If your storage space molds watermelons, don't plant them. If tomatoes need high heat and humidity, don't plant them.

Choose local and tasty variety.

Choosing local and tasty cultivars is the first step to creating a family orchard. If you're new to gardening, investigate fruit trees and contact local experts (like other gardeners) to make this easier. Fruit flavor is extremely essential!

Plant now!

Plant your own fruit plants now that you know how!

Shop for seeds. Walmart and Home Depot sell seeds. If feasible, acquire enough for both kinds of fruit trees—a combination will offer you additional harvest season alternatives!

Take an old shoebox and cut holes on each side large enough for your seedlings' roots but tiny enough so they won't fall through later (as mine did). This homemade greenhouse will keep them warm until next spring!

Growing food is essential for off-grid survival.

Growing food is essential for off-grid survival. It's also a terrific opportunity to educate your kids about food and save money.

Grow fruits and veggies in your garden or apartment balcony. If it grows in your climatic zone (check here), it will probably grow on your yard/apartment balcony!

Climate matters.

Plan your family orchard for your climate. If it's warm and sunny, you can produce more fruit than if it's always chilly and snowy. Before choosing plants, consider the area available for trees and shrubs.

Consider these variables while selecting fruits to plant:

- Fruit size
- Each plant's sunshine needs (leaf light).
- Choose local-hardy trees.
- Check the plants' hardiness before establishing your orchard. The USDA's hardiness zone map may assist.
- Choose cold-tolerant, pest-resistant fruit trees for your survival garden.
- Choose heavy-bearing, small-fruited types.
- Choose heavy-bearing, small-fruited types. Smaller fruit is simpler to pick and store, so fewer trees will feed your family for a year.

Grapes are ideal for this since they grow in many regions and produce a lot of fruit in one season (without trimming).

Choose long-maturing trees.

Know how long fruit plants take to produce. Depending on species and variation, trees mature at different times. Some apple cultivars produce fruit in two years, while others take 15 years!

- Group fruit trees together.
- If you're cultivating fruit trees, group them. This will improve pollination and harvest. Some examples:
- One crabapple and one normal apple tree (or other mix)
- Four cherry trees: Bing, Montmorency, Van/Amarelle, and Balaton/Zweigelt.
- Place the correct tree.
- Choose a climate-appropriate tree to cultivate fruit trees in your garden.
- Consider what fruit grows best in your area:
- Grapes are frost-resistant and may be grown in pots in California and Florida, where winters are cold and summers are hot.

If you reside in a place like Colorado with short growing seasons and frigid nights year-round or have limited space, dwarf apple trees yield smaller harvests but start producing fruit sooner than conventional types.

Apple selection follows

Plant trees in April, then dig them up after they become dormant and the ground freezes.

Plant trees between February and April. Planting while their leaves are just emerging from their buds avoids damage from frost or other severe weather. If you plant in early spring, water your trees until they're established otherwise, they may perish before summer!

After choosing a location for your family orchard and digging a hole for each tree (making sure there are no rocks), fill it with soil enriched by manure or composted leaves to improve fruit quality over time, then carefully place each new addition so its roots don't become exposed above ground level.

A family orchard may boost self-sufficiency.

If you prepare ahead, a family orchard may help you become more food self-sufficient!

Planting an orchard requires some planning. Choose local plants and fruits first. Next, consider how much room you have for planting the trees and how much water they'll need in their first year or two (some trees demand more care than others). Finally, make sure there's adequate place for other crops like vegetables or grains. This may involve modifying what fruit trees are planted to fit together.

Choosing a suitable fruit tree
Before planting, decide where to put your trees. Climate, soil, and space are important while choosing fruit plants.

Your fruit tree species needs a suitable environment. If you reside in a cold climate like most of Canada, citrus and avocado trees may not be able to produce fruit for you since their growth season is too short.

Choose a tree based on climate.
Climate should influence tree choice. Choose weather-resistant trees if you live near the seaside or mountains. Choose family orchard trees based on property size. Grow shrubs instead of trees if it's too tiny for fruit-bearing plants!

Fruit plants for no-grid families
- Apple
- Apricot
- Cherry (sweet-sour)
- Peach
- Plum

Apples are disease-resistant and delectable! They're perfect for your family orchard. Apples can thrive in many soil types and climates, making them one of the simplest fruits to cultivate.

Apple trees suit most backyards. You may start with one tree, but plant two or three types to enjoy a variety of apples throughout the season (and store them for winter!).

Pears and apricots are good for cooking and drying, while apples are harder.

Winter deciduous pears lose their leaves. Plant them in broad sun in most climates. Pears have a short growth season and develop fast (typically within two years), making them unsuitable for long-term subsistence farming. However, pears make amazing jams, jellies, and sauces, and they taste terrific fresh! Apricots taste great fresh or dried into fruit leathers, although there are fewer kinds than apples (perhaps this will improve).

Your garden can survive without power!

A family orchard is one of the finest methods to maintain a consistent supply of fruit and vegetables. Kids may learn about gardening by helping water and select the food.

Without power, your garden must survive!

Family orchards are perfect for off-grid survival. It's crucial.

Your own food supply will offer you piece of mind and guarantee your family gets nutritious meals every day.

Start with one fruit tree and grow.

My orchard has eight apple trees. Three years after moving here, I planted another one. I planted two pears and two plums with my second set of apples, totaling 10 trees. We added five more apple trees last year! If you want to build an orchard but aren't sure how many trees to plant, don't worry! Start small and add fruit variety and space as required.

Graft your own trees to produce additional types.

Graft trees to develop additional types. Grafting joins two wood pieces to grow together. Apple, pear, and other fruit trees may be used. Grafting combines the best traits of several kinds to maximize fruit production.

Rows simplify watering, weeding, and harvesting.

Dig rows using a spade or shovel. Plant the seedling in a 15cm hole. To avoid competition for space and nutrients as plants develop, provide adequate spacing between them!

Remember your trees' roots too! Mulch and mound dirt around each tree to prevent winter damage.

Try kinds that don't grow well locally or on your property. Find a new favorite fruit or nut!

I planted eastern North American Pawpaw (Asimina triloba) trees. It grows well here and produces tons of fruit, but I don't like them since they taste and feel different from other fruits. Try these if you haven't!

When establishing an orchard, space trees so they can grow. This will also simplify pruning and picking.

If you want every fruit tree to receive light and rain, put them in a grid. This works well for smaller orchards with fewer trees. If you're creating a large orchard, put your apple trees wider apart so they can grow and develop without competing for sunshine and water.

Planting fruit-bearing trees around your house is a simple method to preserve your family's survival food supply and provide shade on hot days! They'll supply fresh fruit year-round and keep things cool in summer's 90+ degrees Fahrenheit (32 degrees Celsius).

Orchards are large projects.
Growing an orchard is a significant effort, but it may be successful once established. Find some fruit trees your family likes to start. Your area's abandoned trees are fantastic possibilities!

Ask local farmers or nurserymen what fruit grows best in your area. They may recommend kinds that flourish in their environment and advise you on how to care for them at home!

Plant a garden.
Even in small spaces, gardens may generate food. Gardens may be planted year-round! Remember that many seed banks online sell heritage seeds from throughout the globe at affordable costs (sometimes even free!).

Fruit tree seeds.
If you want additional fruit trees in your yard, gather seeds. Here's how:

Collect seeds six weeks after bloom once the tree has matured its fruit and shed its seeds. When this occurs, check for brown specks on the fruit's surface or feel the juicy pulp for hard tiny balls. Probably seeds! If you're not sure what sort of tree you have, go online for photographs of its fruits around harvest time.

After birds, squirrels, or people have eaten all their fruits, remove any leftover bits from branches so it looks good again without being dirty or unkempt."

- Soil test.
- Before planting an orchard, you must test the soil.
- Soil testing reveals:
- If your soil contains a lot of phosphorus but not enough nitrogen (or vice versa), you should add additional fertilizers to your garden beds before planting.
- To ensure optimum plant development and health, how much organic matter should be supplied each year?

Orchard-style planting.
Planting your trees in an orchard shape will maximize space and ensure that your fruit trees get enough sunlight.

Prepare soil for planting.
First, prepare your soil by mixing in compost and natural fertilizers like manure or blood meal (keep these away from young plants' roots). You can also add lime, but it will take time to break down and release its nutrients.

In arid locations, water new plants.

Water fruit trees and other plants well in their first year or two to help them develop strong roots that can withstand drought.

Grow your own food to live.
Growing your own food on a modest scale may save you money and help you live.

Many techniques exist to produce food without electricity or other resources.

I hope you've learned how to grow a family orchard for no grid survival. This is one of the most basic ways to survive off the grid, and anyone can do it regardless of location or climate. Fruit trees provide delicious food and require less work than traditional gardens because they don't need weeding.

Book 4: How to do Animals and Poultry Breeding

One of the most important things to do in no grid survival is to breed animals and birds. You can start your own rabbit family with a male and a female rabbit. Breeding rabbits is one of the easiest ways to start a new animal family. Ducks are another great animal to breed because they lay eggs every day and eat bugs, which can help you become more self-sufficient. Chickens are also good to breed because they lay eggs and can be used for both meat and eggs. If you want milk or meat in the long run, you can breed goats. Just make sure they have enough food and room first. In order to survive off the grid, you need to do more than just stock up on guns. You also need to farm and raise animals.

Why raise animals and chickens?

The main reason people raise animals and birds is to get food. The less you need to hunt, the more you have.

Another good thing about having a lot of animals is that they can guard you from predators like wolves and bears. If you're afraid about people coming onto your land without your permission, a pack of dogs would make a great guard dog, and chicken coops can be used as alarms.

Different ways to breed.

You can get new animals and birds by breeding them. There are different ways to breed, but the end effect is always the same: an egg that can later hatch into a bird or animal.

You can breed an animal by putting two adults of the same species or different species together, or by putting an adult animal with a baby of the same species. When you try to breed them, it's important that at least one partner has a heart above its head. This means they are ready to breed.

How to Start a Chicken Farm?

There are many ways to get chickens to have babies. The first thing you need to do is set up the place where your chickens will mate. You will need a big pen or coop with lots of room for them to move around and lay their eggs.

When chickens mate, it's important for them to have privacy because they can make a lot of noise! If you can, make sure that your neighbors can't see into your coop or pen. If they see what's going on inside, it could be embarrassing!

How to Breed Rabbits?
It's not hard to breed rabbits, but you need to know what you're doing and have some experience.

Rabbits eat plants and can eat hay, grass, and veggies. They also need clean water to drink all the time.

About 30 days pass during a rabbit's pregnancy, so if you want your bunnies to have babies this year, you need to start right away.

How Do You Breed Goats?
The goat is an animal that has been kept as a pet for a very long time. They are one of the most popular farm animals in the world. Only cattle and pigs are more popular. Goats can be bred at any time of the year, but spring and summer are the best times.

A goat's pregnancy lasts between 145 and 150 days, or 5 months, and the average number of kids born is between 1 and 4. When raising goats, it's important to keep good records so you know how long each pregnancy lasts and how many kids were born each time.

How Do You Raise Pigs?
Pigs can be raised in a number of different ways. You can raise them for their meat, milk, or eggs. They are very good at making meat and eggs and are a great way to get food when you need it.

Putting two pigs in the same pen lets them mate and have babies. The average number of days between mating and giving birth is 114, but this can change based on the type of pig being bred.

After this time, you will have some babies that will stay with their mother until they are big enough to live on their own without her help.

How Do You Breed Sheep?

Sheep are one of the most easy-to-breed animals. The wool, meat, and milk they give are also very useful. To get wool from sheep, you have to make sure they have enough food and water. If you don't have any other way to get food or water, now might be a good time to start thinking about how much land each animal needs each day.

Sheep's wool can be used as a raw material to make yarns, which can then be made into clothes like jackets or socks. You can also use their milk to make things like cheese, yogurt, etc.

Picking The Best Animals To Breed

When you choose your breeding stock, there are a few things to think about.

The first is each animal's gender. So that they can breed, you need an equal number of males and females. If you only have one of each, you can only have one baby animal per birth cycle.

The second thing to think about is whether or not the animals will be able to grow their own food on their own or if they will need help from people to not only live but also thrive.

How to Get Cattle to Breed?

A cow gives birth to one kid at a time. It takes nine months for a cow to give birth. The calf can start eating solid food as soon as it is born, but until its teeth come in, its mother will still need to be milked.

Getting wool from alpacas by breeding them

You can make a little extra money by breeding alpacas for their hair. Alpaca wool is very soft and can be used to make clothes and blankets, among other things. Alpacas are also known for being calm, which makes them easy to work with. Alpacas can be bred at any time of the year, but you shouldn't do it when the weather is too hot or too cold because it can be bad for the health of both the parents and the babies.

If a breeder wants to start their own breeding program, they should buy at least two female alpacas that are at least a year old. Males don't need to be bought separately because they are usually kept with females until they reach adulthood, which takes about two years. Your herd will need a lot of space. At least 5 acres per adult female will give them enough room to move around and make sure that everyone has access to food and water without having to fight over resources like grasses growing on hilltops near riverside pastures, where runoff from the rain makes the soil rich and perfect for growing healthy plants.

Rabbits are bred for their meat and wool.
- Rabbits are a good choice for making meat and wool. They can be raised in cages or pens, but they need a lot of room to move around and fresh air.
- It's easy and cheap to breed rabbits, but if you want to do it properly, you'll need to buy some tools.
- Goats can be raised as livestock or as pets.

If you want to raise goats as animals or as pets, you need to know a few things.

First, goats like to be with other goats because they are group animals. If you plan to leave them alone in your backyard, they will be unhappy and might get mean to people. Second, they don't have many food preferences (they'll eat almost anything), but they always need fresh water. If there isn't any where they live, someone needs to bring them buckets of water every day. Third, when it's time to breed, male goats can be very aggressive toward each other. If this happens in your own family, it could cause serious problems between siblings who get along well otherwise. Make sure everyone knows what's going on before you bring new goats home.

- One of the most important things to do in no grid survival is to breed animals and birds. This will help you have a steady amount of food, which you and your family need.
- Care for the animals, make sure they are fit enough to have babies, and get them ready to mate with other animals of the same type or breed.
- You can start your own rabbit family with a male and a female rabbit.

- Rabbits are easy to take care of, and they are also useful because they will have many babies for you over the course of their lives.

If you already have a place for the rabbits to live, all you need to give them is hay or straw to eat and a bowl of water every day or two. The hardest part of having rabbits is keeping track of when they get pregnant so you know when to separate the males and females so they don't start breeding again right away.

Breeding rabbits is one of the easiest ways to start a new animal family. It doesn't take much time, room, or money, so it's great for living off the grid. Rabbits are also easier to take care of and feed than animals like cows or pigs.

Rabbits have a lot of babies, so if you have enough females in your group, there will always be some kids around.

Ducks

Ducks are another great animal to breed because they lay eggs every day and eat bugs, which can help you become more self-sufficient. If you need meat, you can also get it from ducks. However, you should wait until the ducklings are at least eight weeks old to eat them because their bones aren't fully formed yet.

There is a lot of protein in duck eggs, so if you have a group of ducks, this is a great way to add something healthy and tasty to your diet.

Chickens are also good to breed because they lay eggs and can be used for both meat and eggs.

You can also use chickens to feed your plants, which will help you grow more food.

Breeding goats

If you breed goats, you can get milk and meat from them over time. Just make sure they have enough food and room first.

Breeding goats is the best way to get an animal that will feed you in the long run. They are easy to take care of, and they can have up to two babies a year.

It's not just about getting guns; you also have to farm and raise animals.

In a survival situation, animals are one of the best ways to get food because they can be killed for their meat, milk, and eggs. They take up less space than crops, so this is something to think about if you want to live off the grid in a city where room is limited.

Get some chickens. Chickens are one of the easiest animals to take care of because they don't need much attention once they're set up right (they'll need a safe place to live). Since they give you eggs every day, you'll never be hungry again. Just make sure you have enough feeders and waterers so that none of your plants go hungry or thirsty during the winter months when there isn't much sun due to climate change affecting temperature levels globally causing seasons like winter to be shorter than usual making plants less likely to grow well without proper lighting conditions like candles, torches, etc.

Peafowl

Peafowl are a type of pheasant known for their long tails and beautiful feathers. They can be raised in captivity, but their eggs have to be kept warm by humans.

Peafowl have been around since ancient times, and in 1260, the Chinese ruler Kublai Khan kept one as a pet. Today, there are more than 30 known types of peafowl. However, only peacocks and peahens (females) are usually used for breeding.

Peafowl are pheasants, so they are in the Phasianidae family. They come in many colors, like white, blue, and green with black spots that make them look like they are wearing mascara.

Guinea Hens

If you want to raise chickens without electricity or water, Guinea hens are a good choice. They are also called beautiful birds because of how pretty they look. Guinea hens have been kept as pets since at least 5000 BC. They were first raised in Africa and Asia. They were brought to Europe by traders. Because of their beauty and the fact that they could lay eggs all year long, they were popular pets among royalty.

Guinea Hens needs less space than other breeds of chicken (about 1/2 square foot per bird), but they still need shelter from weather conditions like rain or extreme heat/cold during the winter months when they can't be let out into an enclosed pen area outside like larger chickens can easily do.

Geese

You should add geese to your group. They are easy to take care of, and you can eat the eggs they lay. Geese will also keep pests like foxes and rats away from your farm.

Geese need a lot of space to move around, so the best place to keep them is in an open area where they can eat grass, bugs, and other food. If you live near water or in a wet area with plenty of food all year (like a swamp), geese might be a good choice for you.

Doves and pigeons

The easiest animals to raise are pigeons and doves. They can be kept in captivity, so if you want to start a group of these birds without thinking about having enough food for them, keep them inside until they start laying eggs. Pigeons lay two eggs at a time and sit on them for about two weeks before they hatch. During this time, it's important to give the nest food and water and keep predators away. It's also important not to move the nest too much or you might scare off the mother pigeon.

After they hatch, pigeon chicks grow quickly. After just three months, they are big enough to eat. The best way to raise baby pigeons is to give them milk from another animal, like cows or goats. If you don't do this, you may need to try samples from several different species until you find one that works well enough as both food and milk source.

One of the best ways to make sure you have food after a disaster is to breed your own animals and fowl. It's too bad that it's also one of the most labor-intensive ways to make food. In this chapter, we'll talk about how to do it right so that you can get all the rewards with as little work as possible.

First, you should know that there are two ways to breed: natural (or "wild") reproduction and artificial insemination (AI). AI involves using tools like syringes and semen collection to help fertilization. Natural reproduction is exactly what it sounds like: animals will mate on their own, without any help from humans.

Joining the local club of 4-H or another group like it is one way to learn about breeding. The main goal of these groups is to teach young people about farming, with a focus on growing animals and chickens. You can join these programs as a young person or as an older helper. They usually hold regular meetings where you can learn how to breed animals and birds on your own land.

You should have a plan for what kinds of animals and birds you will be able to breed. The most important thing is to choose animals that can easily reproduce in the situations you are likely to be in.

Before you decide to breed animals or chickens, you should also think about what resources you have at your location, such as room and water.

You also need to think about which animals are most likely to live in your area. For example, if you live on a farm and have a lot of farmland and pasture, sheep may be the best choice for making meat. If you live in a dry area with little rain or water, goats would be a better choice because they can eat scrub and other plants that don't need much water to grow.

If you're thinking about getting chickens for eggs and maybe as pets, you should think about whether you have enough room for them and their house. This depends on how many chickens you want and how big their pen needs to be.

- Some people would rather take care of small animals.
- Some people like to raise small animals like rabbits and chickens, while others like to raise bigger animals like pigs or cows.
- Before choosing what kind of livestock is best for you, you should know what you want from them.

Book 5: How to do Beekeeping

Beekeeping could be the perfect hobby for you if you want to provide honey for your family without having to go to the store. It's also a simple way to make sure you always have pollen and beeswax on hand. But before you jump into this fun game, it's important to know how to keep yourself safe. Here are some tips on how to keep bees for living off the grid:

Beekeeping isn't just a fun sport.

Beekeeping is one of the best ways to get honey, wax, and propolis that will last for a long time. It also helps you learn more about bees and farming in general.

You can keep bees anywhere as long as you have enough room for your hives and there are flowers close that the bees can eat. Bees can't live without pollen, so this might not be the right sport for you if you live somewhere with no flowers.

Bees are a vital part of our environment.

Bees are an important part of our environment because they pollinate many of the plants that humans eat. Bees are important to our food supply because they pollinate many of the plants and crops, we eat. Without bees, we wouldn't be able to get a wide range of fruits, veggies, and nuts throughout the year. When you look at it this way, you can see why having bees is so important.

Bees do well in a wide range of environments and weather.

Bees do well in a wide range of environments and weather. Honeybees, for example, can live in places as different as warm jungles and the Arctic ice. They are not from North America, but people have brought them there.

There are a few things you need to give bees.

You need to give your bees a few things if you want them to be happy and busy. For instance:

Food: Pollen and syrup are both things that bees need to live. This can be given as honeycomb or sugar syrup, which is made by mixing white (or brown) sugar with water. The amount of sugar to water should be 1 part sugar to 3 parts waters, but you can try different amounts.

Water: Bees don't get their water from rivers or lakes like people do. Instead, they get it from the flowers where they find their food. You can help them stay hydrated by putting some small dishes with clean water near their hives. This way, when they come back from gathering nectar from nearby plants, they can get a fresh drink, as nature intended.

Plants will get pollen from the bees.

Bees are essential to your life. They not only help plants grow, but they also make honey. The bees will spread pollen and nectar on plants, which they will then use to make honey. You can make wine with the honey, or you can just eat it right off the comb.

Bees are a great thing to have.

Bees are a great resource that we should protect for future generations. Bees spread pollen to flowers and fields, which makes food for us. We wouldn't be able to eat trees or veggies without them. They also make honey, which is a tasty item that can be used in many dishes.

Beekeeping is a sport that lets you enjoy having bees without having to do all the work of taking care of them yourself. You will need a pre-built hive box, frames with wax supports on them, queen excluders, and hive cleaners. If you want one queen per hive or two, beeswax foundation sheets for each frame instead of using wax caps from live bees' cells; tools like smoker puffs and a brush for cleaning out old combs before adding new ones; protective clothing like a veil/hood combo and gloves when handling frames so you don't get stung; small buckets for moving frames between hives, preferably made of wood because plastic will melt when exposed to heat;

Obtain a beekeeping suit.

When you're gardening, it's important to wear a beekeeper suit. The bees will think you're one of them and won't sting you. You can buy these clothes at any good store that sells beekeeping supplies or online.

Find out how to stay safe near bees.

You need to know a few things about having bees. First, make sure you have the right kind of bees for your area and environment. Second, if anyone in your family or group has allergies, make sure everyone knows about them so they can take steps (like wearing gloves when handling honeycombs) that are right for them.

Third, if you can and especially if this is your first time having bees, find a guide who knows a lot about it.

Get a honey extractor, frames, and a hive.
You'll need to buy your first hive if you want to start your own beekeeping business. This can be done at any shop that sells gardening tools or online. Make sure to get one with frames and one that can also extract honey.

Get some bees.
There are bees for sale on the web. They can be sent to you, but make sure the seller guarantees that they will arrive alive before you buy them.

- Give sugar syrup to your bees.
- Give sugar syrup to your bees.
- Give pollen cakes to your bees to eat.
- Check the temperature of the queen and the hive.

In order to survive, it's important to keep an eye on how hot or cold your bees are. If you don't, they could die from either being too hot or too cold. As long as you have a temperature on hand, this is easy. Just check them every few days to see if anything needs to be changed, like moving them closer or farther away from their heat source.

- Keeping bees is a simple way to give your family honey without going to the store.
- This can be done anywhere, but if you live off the grid or in a rural place, it's especially helpful.
- Having bees around is a great way to get honey, beeswax, and pollen.

Honey is a valuable resource that can be used to make things taste better or to help people get better. It's also a great way to get energy when you need it the most, and if you store it right in jars with airtight lids or tins with wax seals, it will last for years. Honey can even be used as glue if you need something sweet and sticky. Beeswax is another great thing to have on hand because it can be used to make candles, lip balm (if that's your thing), salves, and so on. Also, it helps keep your hive healthy by making sure dust doesn't get in. If dust got into the bees' home base and wasn't cleaned up, it could hurt the bees over time.

Protein can also be found in bees. It can be hard to get enough protein in your food if you live off the grid. Honey and beeswax, both of which are good sources of protein, can help you solve this problem if you keep bees.

- Beekeeping is a great way to get your hands dirty while also learning useful skills.
- You can find the tools you need to keep bees at a hardware shop or online.

You'll need to have the following:

A set of safety gear that includes a veil and gloves. Bees are animals that can sting, so you need to keep yourself safe from them. When a bee stings you, it hurts for days.

A grill and something to burn, like wood chips or leaves. The smoker is used to calm the bees down so that when you open their hive, they don't swarm around your face. You can also use it to scare other animals away if you're having trouble with them.

Honey helps heal wounds and fights germs very well.
Honey can be used as an antibiotic to keep a cut or scrape from getting sick. Honey has antibacterial qualities that will help keep cuts from getting sick after they have been cleaned and wrapped.

Bee pollen is good for a lot of different things, like asthma and stomach problems. It has also been used to treat cancer, gout, and asthma.

If you know how to keep bees, you might not need them.
Beekeeping is an old skill that has been used for thousands of years and is still used today. It's a great way to get honey without having to worry about anything else. Bees are very important because they pollinate plants, which helps people all over the world grow fruits, veggies, and nuts. But they are also very good at making honey.

Bees are important bugs because they pollinate plants and flowers. They also make honey, which can be used in cooking or as a sweetener. Bees are social animals, which means that they live in groups called colonies. In each colony, there is a queen bee in the middle. The queen lays eggs that hatch into larvae, which are tiny bees. Depending on how old they are, the larvae then turn into worker bees or drone bees.

Worker bees make beeswax when they use their bodies and wings to make wax scales on their abdomens. These scales are then scraped off and made into combs, which are used to store honey, pollen, and eggs for the next generation of bees in "bee boxes."

No grid to keep bees

The best way to keep bees without a grid is to keep bees. Bees are important to the health of any environment, and they can give you honey that you can eat or sell. When people think about having bees, the first thing they want to know is how to start. Well, we'll answer that question right now!

The first thing to do: You'll need a hive, which is a box where bees live. You can buy one or make one yourself from pieces of wood or metal. If you build one yourself, make sure the top has big enough holes for air to flow through. These holes will be used in the winter when the temperature drops so low that the bees can't fly out.

The next step is to decide where to put these hives. Ideally, they should go somewhere shady and close enough to be easy to get to.

What you need to keep bees to live off the grid

You will need a box and frames. The frames are what hold the bees in the hive. Depending on how many bees you want to keep, they come in different sizes.

The next thing you'll need is protected clothes that covers your whole body from head to toe. This should be made of thick material, like canvas or leather, so that it can protect you from stings and bites from insects that might get into your clothes while you're working with them.

You also need some kind of smoker to keep the bees from swarming by making smoke that covers their signals so they can't easily find each other when they try to leave the colony. This keeps the bees from getting angry with each other or with people.

How to keep bees to survive without a grid

Bees are an important part of any farm, and having bees can be a great way to make sure you and others have enough honey. To do beekeeping, you will need:

- A couple of beehive boxes (make sure they are empty)
- A knife or other sharp item to cut off the tops of your hives (a saw would be better but harder to find).
- Some frames and a base (that's where they lay their eggs).

How to keep bees safely for off-the-grid living.

- Keep a close eye on the bees. If you see them getting upset, you should leave the area and call a beekeeper for help.
- When you work with bees or their hives, you should wear safety gear. Getting honey isn't worth putting your health at risk.
- If you're allergic to bee stings, don't keep bees at all. If something goes wrong, it's not worth it!
- Beekeeping can be a fun and satisfying sport, but it's important to know and follow the right safety rules.
- Beekeeping can be a fun and satisfying sport, but it's important to know and follow the right safety rules.

Always put on safety gear: If you want to keep stings from hurting your skin, you must wear gloves, long sleeves, and long pants. You might also want to wear a hat or veil over your face so that bees can't get close enough to sting you in the mouth or eyes.

Only use tools that have been cleaned: To keep bees from getting diseases like varroa mites or tracheal mites, all beekeeping tools must be cleaned well before each use. This is done by boiling them in water for 15 minutes with 1 tablespoon of bleach per gallon. This will kill any germs on them so they don't spread sickness to your colony!

Now that you know how to keep bees and what they need, it's time to get started! You don't even need a big room or a lot of fancy tools. If you have flowers and trees that naturally attract bees, all you need is a small place in your backyard or on your porch where they can live happily.

Book 6: How To Do Hunting And Fishing

I've been a survivor for a long time. I think we should be able to take care of ourselves in case of an accident or disaster. In this world, you can't always count on other people, so it's important to know how to hunt and fish for yourself. In this part, I'll show you how to hunt and fish so you can stay alive without a grid.

Start at the beginning.

For off-grid living, it's important to learn how to hunt and fish, so start with the basics. Before you catch a fish, you should know how to clean it. If you don't know how yet, practice on some dead fish until it becomes easy for you. If you don't have any fresh water handy, you can boil them in salt water instead of letting them go bad in the sun or by leaving them out overnight. This will also help keep their taste.

Once you've mastered these skills, you can move on to bigger things, like learning how long something takes from start to finish. This way, if there's an emergency, you won't waste time trying to figure out what to do next while everyone else stands around waiting impatiently for someone else to decide where to go next, which isn't always easy because people don't always agree on which path is best.

- Make sure you know where you are and what the land is like where you will be shooting.
- Know the place where you plan to hunt. It's important to know what kind of area you'll be shooting in so you can make the right plans. If there are mountains nearby, and bears are also around, it might not be a good idea to shoot an elk standing on top of one of those mountains.
- Know what kinds of animals live in your area and where to find them. How often animals move around and how easy or hard it is for hunters to find them depends on what kinds of animals live there and how many of them there are. For example, you can sometimes find deer near farms where farmers have left food out for them. If there aren't any farms nearby, these deer might not show up as often because they can't get food from people anymore!

Get a map of the area from the ranger station or National Forest office that is closest to you.

Having a map of the place you're driving through is important, especially if you plan to go off-roading. Maps can help you find your way around, and they can also show you where the best places are to fish or hunt. If a national forest office is close, you can ask them for plans of the area.

Don't ever lose track of where you are.

Keep in mind that you always need to know where you are. It's easy to get lost, especially if you don't know the area well or haven't been there in a while. To keep from getting lost, you should always have a watch, GPS device, and plan with you. If you can, use all three tools at the same time so they work better together than when used separately.

Find Rivers and Streams

The first step to hunting and fishing without a grid is to find a stream or river. Streams and rivers can be found in most parts of the country. It's easier to find them if you look for natural signs like big rocks or trees.

Look for man-made waterways like storm drains and sewer systems if you live near a city. These are also great places to catch fish. If there are no nearby pools of water or they are too dirty, try making a small hole on dry ground. You might catch something there!

As soon as you find water, you can start fishing. The best thing to do is just stand still until something bites. If this doesn't work, try slowly moving around while holding bait above your head so that anything below knows where it came from and hopefully comes after.

Find the best place to fish in the water.

Now that you know what to look for, we can talk about the details.

First, you should look for a good place to fish in the water. You can find one of these by looking around your area or town for rivers, lakes, ponds, or streams. If there aren't any natural bodies of water close, you might have to dig a hole yourself! Checking Google Maps is a good way to find out if this is possible. Just zoom in on an area that looks good and see what comes up (hint: it will probably say "Private Property" somewhere).

How to Fish in the Woods for Food

So now you're in the woods. Congratulations! This is a big step toward becoming a whole person who can take care of himself or herself. But there are some things you need to do before you can start building your house or gathering firewood.

First, there's food! If you want to stay alive out here for a long time, you'll need to eat something solid. And trust me, you will. We're lucky that nature gives us a never-ending source of free food right at our feet—or rather, on top of them. It's called fishing, and once you know how to do it, it's very easy:

Choose a place where there are a lot of fish moving around. These places are usually near waterfalls or lakeshores where big rocks stick out into shallow water and smaller fish can hide behind them while bigger fish swim above them looking for food. String or rope can be tied to one end of a pole so that when it is put against something solid, like dirt or sand, it stands up straight and doesn't fall over. Then, hooks can be put on both ends using whatever is available (needle nose pliers work great!).

What are some good foods for hunting?

Here are some of the best shooting foods:

- Deer
- Rabbit
- Raccoon
- Turkey
- Squirrel
- Duck and other birds, like geese, pheasant, and grouse (when in season).

Finding a place to sleep and start a fire

Find a dry place to sleep that is out of the weather. If you need to, you can build a shelter or just dig a hole in the ground. The most important thing is to stay warm and dry at night, because you won't be able to sleep if you're cold or wet when it's time to go to bed.

Make sure your fire pit has some kind of wind break around it so that coals don't get blown away by strong winds or by people blowing on them. Also, make sure there are no dry leaves close that a spark could easily set on fire.

Lastly, know that this isn't just about getting food. It's also about staying warm and safe.

What you need to know to hunt and fish without electricity.

- You need to know what the rules are. Make sure you have permission from the landowner before you hunt on their land.
- You need to know what kinds of fish and animals live in your area so you can catch them without breaking the law (or getting sick).
- You also need to know how to clean your catch the right way, especially if you don't have running water.
- Once all of this is done, you can just cook some tasty food.
- Learn how to hunt and fish to get started.
- You should find out about the different kinds of tools used for shooting and fishing.
- You should also learn where the best places are to hunt and fish.
- Lastly, you'll need to learn how to set up a fishing pole and other things you'll need on your trip through the woods.

Choose a great place.

When picking a hunting spot, you should make sure it's not too far from camp. You don't want to have to go back and forth every day with your catch. The same is true for fishing: you should be able to walk to the water so you don't have to put in extra work just to get food.

When shooting or fishing, you also don't want to be near big bodies of water, which can bring in predators like bears and wolves. If there are people who live near these animals' natural environments, they might also come looking for food. Also, don't set up camp near any homes where humans might be able to find out what's going on in their land. This could lead them right to your camp!

Make your choice.

The first thing you have to do is decide what tool you want to use. There are many different kinds of tools that can be used for shooting and fishing, such as:

- Arrow and bow
- Gun
- Fishing stick (this is probably the best way to do it)
- If you are strong enough, use a spear.
- And finally, there are also traps. Some types of traps are snares and deadfalls.

Find out when it is and what the rules are.

First, find out what kinds of fish and animals live in the area where you want to hunt or fish. This will help you choose the right bait and hook. You can also ask a shooter or fisherman in your area if there are any special rules or times for the season that might apply to your area.

Once you know what animals you can hunt or catch, figure out which ones will be easiest to catch based on the time of year. For example, you might not be able to fish if there is ice on the water.

Find out what kinds of animals and fish

It is important to learn about the fish and animals in the area where you are shooting or fishing. You need to know what kind of bait and hook will draw them and when they are most busy.

Different states have different rules about shooting and fishing, so it's important to do some study before you take your gun or fishing pole out into the wild.

Even if you are off the grid, you can still eat well. Just know what to eat and where to look for it.

You can hunt animals, catch fish, and trap animals.

Fish: Any prepper needs to know how to fish because it's an easy way to get energy that doesn't take much work or time to prepare. You will need some fishing gear, though. To fish, all you need is a stick with a line on one end and food on the other. Once you catch a fish, cut under its gills with a knife or sharp rock to remove its head. Don't eat any part of the fish raw, because it might have bugs. If you can, try to eat cooked meat instead. This will make sure that everything goes down well and no one gets sick.   Animals: Hunting is another great way to get food when you're off the grid, but it takes more skill than fishing, so don't go into the wilderness alone and without any tools.

Hunting

Hunting is an important skill for getting food. You can hunt with a bow and arrow, but it takes time to learn and practice to get good at it. A rifle will make your job much easier, but it's hard to use one well if you don't already know how to use one.

When hunting, you also need a hunting knife to gut the animal (remove its intestines) once you've killed it. If you don't know how to clean an animal properly before skinning it, blood left on the fur could attract predators or scavengers who might attack you when you try to get your catch later.

Fishing

- What is the best way to fish to stay alive?
- How do I use a fishing rod to catch fish?
- How do I catch fish? What kind of food should I use?
- How do I clean the fish I catch, and what should I watch out for when I do?
- If you want to eat the fish you caught, you need to cook them the right way so they don't make you sick or give anyone else food poisoning.

Trapping

Using traps to catch fish, mice, rabbits, and other animals is one of the best ways to get food in a survival situation.

Make a line snare by tying a length of twine around two close trees. Tie one end of the twine around your trap, which can be anything from an empty soda bottle to an old shoe. Leave enough space at the bottom so that when you slide it over the animal's head, its feet will reach down through this opening and rest on either side of your trap or whatever you're using as bait!

To catch rabbits with snares, tie several pieces together as tightly as possible. If you need more strength, add another piece. Make loops every few inches along each piece so that when you're done, they look like small ropes instead of long ones. Then, tie the two ends together to make two large loops that are loose enough to fit rabbits and give them some freedom, but tight enough to catch them without hurting them.

You can live well without a grid if you hunt and fish.

Hunting and fishing are great ways to survive without a grid. You can find food in your backyard or anywhere else. If you have the right tools, you can catch fish with your bare hands! The best time of year to hunt is in the fall and winter, when animals don't move around as much (except bears).

In your garden, you can find food.

Hunting and fishing could be the perfect way to get your family outside and into nature. You don't even have to go far; you can find food right in your own garden!

Many people don't realize this because they don't know what to look for or how to properly identify them. This is why learning about edible plants can be so helpful for survival situations: if you know where certain plants grow naturally, then finding them in an urban environment shouldn't be too hard (and hopefully less dangerous than going out into the wilderness).

You need a good knife to hunt with.

When you're off the grid and in the wilderness, a hunting knife is one of the most important tools to have with you. A good hunting knife should be sharp, easy to carry and use, and able to cut through bone. It should also have a sheath to protect the blade from water or dirt and keep it safe from other people who may want what you have or want to take advantage of your ignorance.

Fall and winter are the best times to go hunting.

The best time to hunt is in the fall. This is because there are fewer animals around in the fall and winter than in the summer, so it's easier to find them and it's safer because there are fewer animals around.

You can make a fishing stick on your own for free.

First, you'll need a stick. The longer and stronger it is, the better. You can find sticks in your backyard or on a walk in the woods. Next, tie one end of your string (or fishing line) around one end of your pole. Then, tie an easy-to-see piece of cloth to that end so you know which end is which. Then, tie another piece of cloth on top of where your hook will go so it will be easy for you and anyone else who wants to use it to

Now it's time for the last step: putting everything together. Use zip ties or tape to connect one piece from each side (one from each end) until they're firmly attached but still flexible enough to move around. This way, they won't break off easily when you're using them outside, like when you're hiking in nature reserves where there aren't any stores nearby and materials like these may cost up to $20 per pack, which would be too expensive if used only once.

Find out where it is

The next step is to find the location. You will need to be able to find your way back there, so make sure it's not too far from home and that you have easy-to-remember landmarks. For example, if you're going hunting in the forest and using trees as landmarks, try to find a tree with an interesting shape or color pattern so it stands out from other trees.

How to Choose the Best Weapons

For hunting, you'll want to use a rifle. Rifles are the best way to kill game, and anyone who knows how to use one can do it. If you don't have access to rifles or don't know how to use them, you can also use a bow. In some situations, bows can work just as well as arrows at longer ranges, but they're harder on your hands.

Using a bow and arrow to hunt and fish

With a bow and arrow, you can hunt animals from a distance. If you don't have a bow, you can make one with simple tools. To make a good hunting tool, use strong wood like cedar or ash that won't warp or rot over time. When you string it, make sure it has enough tension so it won't break when you use it.

If you have fishing poles, spears, or even better, a boat, these will help you catch fish without having to get close to them. If you don't have any other tools, you could also try using nets to catch small animals like frogs or snakes, but be careful not to put too much weight on them because they might break if you try to catch a deer.

How to wash a fish.
- Clean the fish as soon as you catch it.
- Use a sharp knife to cut out the fish's guts.
- Use another sharp knife (or your hands) to cut off the fish's head and tail.
- Wash your newly caught specimen in cold water until all the blood is gone from its body cavity. Then, dry it off with a towel and put it in a cooler with ice or a refrigerator until you're ready to use it.

How to Catch Bigger Fish
There are a few things you can do if you're having problems catching bigger fish. One is to use a bigger hook. If the fish are hitting your bait but not getting caught, try using a bigger hook to get through their teeth and into their mouth.

Next, try using a stronger line instead of a smaller one. This will make it easier for them to feel or see the lure's weight as it goes through the water, which they depend on a lot.

If you've tried everything above and nothing seems to work, you might want to try something completely different. Try using longer poles instead of shorter ones when casting out into open water from shoreline locations like beaches or piers where there may be limited room available due to space constraints that we must work within to successfully complete such tasks without making mistakes.

If you know what to do, you can catch fresh food to eat.
How to Catch a Fish: You will need a fishing stick, a hook, and some food, like worms. When it rains is the best time to go fishing because the fish swim closer to the top and are easier to catch.

How To Clean A Fish: Remove the fish's scales by scraping them off with a knife or filet knife. Rinse the fish under cold water until all traces of blood are gone from its body cavity. Drain well before cooking or freezing any part of the fish's head that has been removed (ears, eyes, etc.) so nothing gets into your stomach when you eat it later. Once the fish is cooked, any scales that are still on it will fall off. If they don't, just scrape it again before eating it right out of the pan.

You can live well without a grid if you hunt and fish. It's easy to learn how to find food in your own backyard. You'll need a good hunting knife, but you can also use traps or bows and arrows. If you know where to look, it won't be hard at all to find fresh meat.

Book 7: How To Do Foraging

Foraging is a fun way to change up what you eat. It lets you get closer to the earth while learning more about plants and nature. Plus, it's a great way to add to your food if you're trying to survive. But before you go out into the wild with a basket and a field guide, make sure you know what you can eat and what you can't. We'll talk about how to start hunting safely in this post, so you can enjoy your new sport without worrying about getting sick.

What is it to forage?

Foraging is the act of gathering wild plants and other things from nature to use as food or medicine. Foraging can be done on a small scale, like for one's own family, or on a bigger scale as part of survivalism. Some wild plants are rare or protected by law in some countries, so it is against the law to take them.

How to find tasty plants in the wild

When you're out in the woods, you probably won't have access to a food store or even your own home. If you want to eat, you'll have to go out into nature and find food. One way to do this is to go out and look for food, but what if we told you, it could be easy?

Finding plants that you can eat is an art that takes practice, but once you get good at it, you can eat for weeks at a time. People can find a lot of information online that tells them how to tell which plants are dangerous and which ones are safe to eat, as well as what parts of each plant are safe to eat. We really think you should check these out before you go into the woods with only an apple tree as a map.

Edible plants

Edible plants are a great place to start exploring because they are often easy to recognize and can be found almost anywhere. Here are a few of the most popular plants that can be eaten:

- Strawberries, raspberries, and blueberries that grow in the wild.
- Nuts (walnuts)
- Vegetables (potatoes)
- Wild foods to eat

- Arugula is a leafy green that can be used in salads, sandwiches, and soups.
- Beechnut: The beechnut is a nut, but it's so small that you can eat it as a snack or add it to your favorite meals.

Blackberries are one of the most popular wild foods in North America and Europe. They're sweet and tasty, but make sure you know how to pick them without getting stung by bees.

Burdock root: This vegetable has been used as both food and medicine for hundreds of years in places like Japan, Korea, and China. It is also good for your health because it is high in vitamin C.

Don't eat anything that you aren't sure of.

Make sure something is safe to eat before you eat it. You can do this by making sure the plant is grown in a place where there are no chemicals or herbicides. It should also be growing near water, like streams or ponds. This means that its roots have been able to reach down into good dirt and get lots of nutrients from it.

Don't eat the plant if you aren't sure about any of these things.

There are many ways to learn about hunting, but a good place to start is by learning the basics of what plants are safe and which ones are dangerous.

Add to a box for bugs.

One of the best ways to find more food is to put more bugs in your bug box. Boxes for bugs can be made out of things like wood and metal wire. Most of the time, they are made from an old shoe box or another type of container, but they can also be made from things found in nature, like leaves or twigs that have dropped.

To make your own bug box, just cut a hole on one side that is about half an inch wide and big enough for bugs to crawl through. Then put dirt from outside on the bottom so that grasshoppers can't get out when they come in. Once that's done, put it near a group of plants where there are lots of caterpillars and beetles, and wait calmly for them to crawl right into your trap!

Get a guide to the area.

You can get a field guide from the library or a small store near you. Before you go out on your own, you should learn about the different kinds of trees so you know what to look for and what to avoid. It also helps to have pictures so you can tell who they are just by looking.

Foraging can be a lot of fun.

hunting is a fun way to add variety to your food, but it can also be dangerous. Before you go hunting, make sure you know what you're doing.

Many people like to go out and look for food on their own. People do get hurt, though, when they go out into nature without a leader or mentor who knows how to do it safely and successfully and try to find food on their own. This part will teach you not only the best ways to go out and find food, but also which plants are safe to eat and which ones aren't.

- Go on a walk to find food.
- Gather what you see.
- Write down what you found and where it grew or was found so you can find it again.
- Find the wild plants near you.
- Find the plants that can be eaten, are dangerous, or are both.
- Learn which parts of the plant are edible and how to cook them.

Know What to stay away from and what to pick

Some things should be avoided, and others should be taken advantage of. For example, you shouldn't eat mushrooms unless you know for sure that they are safe to eat. Some mushrooms look like other types of mushrooms, but they can be dangerous or even deadly.

On the other hand, there are many plants that can be eaten raw or made with little preparation, like dandelion greens, which have a slightly bitter taste, or purslane, which has a spicy taste. You can also find berries on trees in most places. Just make sure they aren't dangerous before you eat them.

Find out how to name each plant.

You'll also have to figure out how to recognize each plant. For example, you can tell what kind of plant it is by the shape and color of its leaves. If your plant has three leaves on one side, it's probably a clover or mint type. Probably sage or rosemary if there are five leaves on one side.

If you know these simple rules, you won't eat something deadly by chance when you're out in the wild. looking for food, and believe me, there are a lot of things that look like food but aren't safe to eat!

Find out how to make a drying rack

If you don't have a dehydrator or other tools, drying your food is a great way to keep it fresh. You can use twigs or sticks to make a drying rack, and you can use clay to make an oven.

Make sure your drying rack is made of the right kind of wood: Look for woody trees that have been dead for at least two years, like oak or maple. The longer they've been dead, the better. When exposed to water, hard woods like oak are less likely to bend than soft woods like pine.

Make sure there is enough airflow around each piece of food that you are drying: If there isn't enough airflow around the food being dried, mold will grow on it instead of letting it dry out properly! To fix this, just add more cross-pieces to your homemade drying racks so that there's enough space between each piece drying so that nothing grows on them while they're baking in their little ovens!

- Before you eat them, make sure you know what they are.
- You should be able to tell what plants you're picking and make sure they're safe to eat.
- Before you eat them, make sure they are not dangerous or harmful.
- Don't forget to look at the plant's roots as well as its leaves and flowers. They might also have some good stuff on them.

Learn about plants that look like ones that are deadly.

You need to know the difference between plants that are harmful and plants that can be eaten. Most of the time, people who go out to find food make the mistake of mistaking a plant that isn't edible for one that is.

Poison hemlock, for example, has leaves that look like wild carrot or Queen Anne's lace, but if you eat them, they will kill you! If you're not sure if a plant is safe to eat, don't eat it until you're sure it won't make you sick or, worse, kill you.

You should also learn about plants that are dangerous to eat raw but are safe to eat when cooked. Acorns and wild greens are two examples of these.

Find out which wild plants are safe to eat in the spring and summer, and which are safe to eat in the fall and winter, when they are not growing.

Find at least one plant that can be eaten in each of these groups:

- Trees
- Shrubs/brambles
- Herbs/flowers/leaves

You should also learn how to spot dangerous plants so you can stay away from them.

Learn about the seasons so you can tell which plants are growing and what they look like at different times of the year. If you know this, you'll be able to find tasty plants where they grow naturally.

Learn how to find your way around.
In order to survive, you need to know the basics of direction. Without a cell phone, you can figure out where you are on the earth's surface by figuring out which way is north, south, east, and west. This will help you figure out how to leave a place or get back to it after a trip.

It's important to remember that there are many ways to do this. This is just one example of how it can be done using both natural things (like the sun) and man-made things (like compasses or GPS devices).

If you know what to look for and how to tell it apart,

If you know what to look for and how to recognize it, you'll be better able to take care of yourself if something goes wrong while you're out.

Learning about the plants in your area is the best way to start. You can do this by taking a lesson on the topic or reading books about it. There are also apps that can help guide you through some of them and give you information about where they grow best. This makes it easy for me to know where to look first in my neighborhood (or anywhere else) if an emergency comes up.

Find out which plants and mushrooms you can eat.

This is the most important thing you can do if you need to stay alive. You don't want to eat just any plant or vegetable. You want to make sure you're eating something good for your body, not something that will hurt it. So go out and start figuring out what things are! Don't worry if it takes a while. Learning about plants and mushrooms that you can eat takes practice, but once you know what they look like in their natural state (and where they grow), it should be easy to find them even if you don't have grid power.

Know where you are.

It's important to know where you are when you're out exploring and looking for things. You never know when you'll find something helpful!

If there are plants that you can eat close, don't pick them all. Leave some behind so they can grow back and be used again (or by someone else) in the future. You should also avoid eating wild mushrooms unless an expert says they are safe. Some mushrooms look the same, but some of them are poisonous and can make you sick or kill you if you eat them.

Practice, practice, practice!

Practice, practice, practice! You can't just read a book about food plants and expect to know what they look like. You need to go out into the wild and learn by doing. When you do this, make sure you are always aware of your surroundings and don't hurt any animals or plants while you learn which ones are safe to eat.

Go to the wild food shop near you.

This is the best place to start if you are lucky enough to live near a wild food store. Most of these shops sell dried herbs and spices that are great for your prepper pantry. You can also buy fresh greens like nettles and dandelion leaves, but they might be more expensive than getting them at your local store or farmers market.

How do you find it now that you know what to look for?

The best thing to do is to go with a group of people who know how to forage. So, they can show you where different kinds of food are and how to find them. If there aren't any groups near you or if they're busy (which is usually the case), try looking online for information on local clubs or organizations that might be able to help.

Foraging can support a survival diet

Foraging is a great way to get extra food, but it's not a replacement for other ways of getting food. You'll need more than just wild plants and seeds to stay alive in the long run. Fish and game animals, like bunnies, are good sources of energy.

Why is it important to gather food?

Foraging means going out into nature to look for food. Foraging can be done to add to the food you already have, or it can be used as your main source of food.

Foraging is a great way to get food if you don't have any tools and don't have much time to learn. This is especially true for people who live off the grid or can't get food from other sources.

Book 8: Ways to Reduce Waste and Save Money

I'll tell you the truth: I hate to waste money. It's not even just about saving money; it's about using the resources we have in a more sensible way. So, there are lots of ways we can save money and reduce waste in our homes by making smart choices when we shop and by using things we already have. Here are some easy ways to reduce the amount of trash you make and save some money:

Take a look at your garbage.

By looking at your trash, you can figure out where you're making the most trash. This will help you figure out what you need to do to cut down on waste and save money. One great way to do this is to divide your trash into three groups: food waste, recycling, and things that go in the trash (like plastics).

Use less packing.

Buy in bulk. The idea is easy, but it works. You can save money by getting more of the things you use most often. Try shopping at a bulk food store or co-op instead of your local grocery store if you live near one.

By reusing glass jars and containers as much as you can, you can cut down on the amount of packing you use for packaged goods. For example, instead of buying new plastic wrap every time your current roll runs out (and then putting away all that extra plastic), put any scraps in an old yogurt container with a lid or a plastic baggie that you can seal. You'll save money and space!

- Make your own goods to clean.
- Switch out harmful, one-time-use personal care things with ones you can reuse.
- Use reusable water bottles, plates, and other items instead of ones you have to throw away.

You can also cut down on waste by reusing water bottles, plates, and other items instead of throwing them away. This can be especially helpful if you're going to be away from home longer than normal. Things that can be used again are usually made of plastic or glass and can be put in the washing, so they will last longer than things that are meant to be thrown away.

- Turn off lights and machines when you don't need them to save energy.
- When you leave a room, turn off the lights.
- Turn off your computer and phone charger when they are not being used.
- When you turn off lights, machines, and tools that aren't being used, you can save up to 50% of the energy you would have wasted.

If you want to save money and trash less, the first thing you should do is stop buying foods that come in plastic containers. This includes cheese and products for which there is no obvious way to buy them without plastic.

You might think it's okay because some plastic products can be recycled, but that's not always the case. For example, most kinds of yogurt won't be accepted by your local recycling program because they have too much wetness (which can lead to mold growth) or they have metal lids that can't be separated from the rest of the materials being recycled. Also, many places have banned single-use plastic bags because they hurt wildlife and sea life. However, if you buy food with these materials connected, you'll have to use the same bags every time.

You can reduce waste by choosing what you buy and how you use it more wisely.

- Don't use too much packing. Waste from packaging is a big problem, so try to buy things that come in less packing or none at all, like bulk food.
- Whenever you can, buy things in bulk. This saves money and cuts down on the number of one-time-use plastic packages that end up in dumps every year. If you have to buy packed foods or drinks, look for ones that come in reused containers, like glass bottles, instead of plastic bottles that you have to throw away. You can then use those containers again.
- Use handkerchiefs instead of paper towels, toilet paper rolls, and napkins to cut down on waste. Handkerchiefs are just as good at

cleaning up messes, and you can wash them between uses if you need to (just don't put them in your laundry box!). You'll also save money, since handkerchiefs are usually cheaper than their throwaway cousins and do the same job of keeping us clean.

Use a holder for plastic bags.

If you don't already use reusable bags, it's time to start. You can get them at almost any grocery store or large retailer. They come in all shapes and sizes, from canvas totes to plastic shopping pouches. They're great for carrying groceries home from the store and other things like clothes or toys when you're traveling.

You can also find bag holders online that keep your reusable bags neat and organized in your trunk or car so they're easy to grab when you need them (and save space). These are especially helpful if you forget what's in there until after the first use, or if someone else drives most of the time.

Get a bin for compost

Set it up in your lawn or find a community garden near you to use the bins there. If you have room, time, and don't mind getting dirty, think about starting your own community garden!

Buy a filter for your water.

Use the same water filter for everything, or buy more than one. One with a built-in filter is best, but you can also use it as a bottle or tap adapter if you need to. This way, you won't have to keep buying new filters every time they run out, which will happen fast.

Learn how to store food in bulk so you can live off the grid.

If you buy food in bulk, make sure to store it properly so it doesn't go bad. If you don't have a refrigerator or freezer, there are a few things you can do to keep your food from going bad.

Get creative with sealed containers. You can use plastic bags or Tupperware containers with tight-fitting lids. Just make sure they aren't cracked or broken in any way, because they won't be able to keep wetness out if they have holes in them.

Freeze it: This method works best for foods that don't need to stay frozen for long periods of time, like ice cream. Freezing will also help preserve meats, dairy products, and fruits and vegetables that might go bad faster than others because they contain a lot of water, like strawberries.

Switch to bulk stacks of toilet paper.

If you want to reduce your waste, you could switch from toilet paper to bulk stacks of newspaper. This can be an effective way to cut down on the amount of trash that ends up in landfills. If you don't like this idea or don't want to learn how to use a squatty potty, there are other ways to save money and reduce your household's carbon footprint.

- Make your own beauty products at home with things you already have.
- You can save money and cut down on waste by making your own beauty items.
- You can make lotions, soaps, shampoos, and conditioners at home with simple items like coconut oil and herbs. This is much cheaper than buying lotions, soaps, shampoos, and conditioners at the store, and they will last longer because they don't have preservatives.
- Cut down on, re-use, and trash.
- Think of ways to make sure you don't make as much trash in the first place.
- Instead of throwing things away, try to find new ways to use them.
- What you can't reuse or cut down on, recycle!

Composting

Composting is a great way to turn your food scraps into good soil for your garden. You can compost in an open pile or in a compost bin. If you have room, consider building your own compost bin out of recycled materials like pallets or old fencing panels. The key is to make sure the materials are breathable so air can flow through them and help break down the waste faster than if it were just sitting in a pile on top of dirt.

Consider using slow-release fertilizers instead of quick-release ones like Miracle-Gro. These will last longer and be easier on plants over time because they don't burn them with too much nitrogen all at once. This is especially important for veggie plots.

Grow the food you eat.

Growing your own fruits, veggies, and herbs is a great way to save money and reduce waste. You can do this in pots or even on a porch.

If you grow your own food, you will have access to fruits and vegetables that are fresher than if you bought them at the store. You will also know exactly what went into growing your food, since no pesticides or chemicals were used.

Repair and reuse broken things

Fixing broken things is a great way to save money and reduce waste. If you have an old lamp that needs a new cord or your TV stopped working and you can't afford to buy a new one, there are many things you can do instead of throwing the whole thing away.

If you're good with electrical wiring or know someone who is, you might be able to fix it yourself instead of buying a new one. You might also try buying a cheap replacement part online so you don't have to replace the whole thing if you don't have to. For example, if your laptop screen breaks but the rest of the computer still works, you could buy a new screen for your laptop online.

Use water bottles and coffee mugs that you can reuse.

If you're going to buy bottled water, look for a brand that has a smaller carbon footprint or is more environmentally friendly. For example, Aquafina uses less plastic than Dasani and comes in a lightweight package made from 35% plant-based materials (the rest of its bottle is still made of plastic). Life factory's glass bottles aren't zero waste, but they can be recycled.

Use the shower less.

Showers are a great way to relax and feel better, but they can also waste a lot of water. The average American uses about 17 gallons (64 liters) of water per day in the shower, which is more than half of what a household uses. If you're looking for ways to save water, this is a good place to start.

Try these tips to save money on your water bill and cut down on waste:

- Turn off the shower while you are soaping up or rinsing off. This will save water and energy. You may even want to install low-flow showerheads that use less hot water but still feel great on your skin.
- Make a list of what you need to buy and stick to it when you go food shopping.
- If you want to buy something but don't need it right away, wait until your next shopping trip and check to see if it's still on sale.
- When you can, buy in bulk, but not if it means you have to store a lot of food.
- You can save money and reduce trash by getting less new stuff and fixing or finding new uses for the things you already have.
- Fix broken things instead of buying new ones. If you have an old appliance that doesn't work anymore, don't throw it away! Look up how to fix it on YouTube or ask around for help from friends who know about that kind of thing. You might be surprised at how easy some repairs are, like if the cord is frayed, all it takes is a little electrical tape to make it like new again!
- Use reusable containers instead of plastic bags or other disposable packaging when you go grocery shopping. Even better, grow your own food. This can save you money in a few ways. First, you won't have to pay extra because of the extra weight of all those plastic bags. Second, buying fruits and vegetables that aren't packaged together means they'll last longer and won't go bad.

Use less plastic.

Plastic is everywhere, and it's not going away any time soon. The best way to use less plastic is to use reusable items instead of disposable ones. For example, if you buy a piece of fruit at the store, bring an old jar to put it in instead of getting a new one each time. If you're buying milk or juice from the store, bring your own reusable bottle instead of getting one from them (and then throwing it away).

Shopping without plastic

If you're ready to make the switch, the first step is to get rid of all the plastic bags and containers in your home. You can do this by buying reusable items like cloth produce bags and glass jars that can be used over and over again.

Cloth napkins can be used instead of paper towels to clean up messes and dry food in a way that is better for the environment.

If you cut up old t-shirts, you can use them as rags to do things like clean windows or wipe down tables after cooking. Just make sure the pieces aren't too big.

Avoid single-use things

Next time you are at the store, look at what you have in your cart. If there are any single-use items, put them back and find an option. Plastic bags, straws, and water bottles are some of the most common single-use items that end up in landfills and cause pollution all over the world.

There are many options that can help you cut down on waste and save money:

- Use reusable shopping bags instead of plastic or even paper ones. You can buy these at most grocery stores or make them yourself out of old shirts or pants.
- Bring your own water bottle with you when you go out; most places have free refilling spots.
- When you go to the food store, bring your own bags and packages.
- Bring your own shopping bags to the store to cut down on the number of plastic bags you use.
- If you buy a lot of food, consider buying reusable containers to store leftovers and bulk foods. This is better for the environment than buying throwaway plastic containers, especially if they can't be recycled (check with your city or county).

Bring your own bottle of water when you go out to eat.

- Bring your own water bottle to places to avoid using throwaway cups and reduce the amount of trash that ends up in landfills.
- You can also bring your own bags when you go grocery shopping, which will help you waste less food altogether.

- You can either compost food scraps at home or find a recycling service in your area.
- Composting is an easy way to reuse food scraps and reduce waste in landfills. You can learn more about composting at home or find a local program that accepts food scraps, like your city's curbside pickup service.

Learn how to make your own cleaning materials out of things you find in nature.

The internet is a great source of information, but it's also full of false information. The best way to learn how to make your own cleaning products is to actually do it. Start with something simple, like homemade laundry soap or all-purpose cleaner, and then move on to more complicated things.

It can be easy to take steps to waste less and save money.

Reduce the amount of food you throw away. When you buy too much, it goes bad before you can use it all. This is especially true with fruits and vegetables. If you buy more than you need and don't eat the rest within a few days, it will go bad before you know it.

Buy only what you need for one meal at a time. If a recipe calls for two onions instead of one, cut the onion in half and use only half. Don't throw away the other half! You'll save money by not throwing away food that has gone bad because you bought too much.

Extra amounts of leftovers or cooked items (like soups or stews) can be frozen. This way, they won't go bad before their time again.

- You can make your own toothpaste.
- There are a few ways to make your own toothpaste, but they all use things you can find in your home.
- Make a paste by mixing baking soda, water, and peppermint oil in a bowl until it's thick enough.
- Use this paste on your toothbrush as usual. If you don't like the taste, add more water until it's right for you.
- Keep in a jar that keeps out air for up to 6 months.

- You can make your own cleaning soap.

If you want to save money and cut down on waste, making your own laundry soap is a simple way to do both.

There are only two things you need: borax and washing soda. You can find both of these things at most grocery stores or hardware stores, or you might already have them in your pantry. They're also very cheap: a box of each will cost less than $10, which will make enough detergent for dozens of loads of laundry and will last for months.

This recipe works well with both standard top-loading machines and HE front-loading machines because it doesn't have any water softeners or fabric softeners, which can cause problems with some types of washing.

Use cloth diapers and wet wipes.
Cloth diapers and wipes are a great alternative to disposable ones. They're better for the environment, save you money, and are easier on your baby's skin.

You can clean pacifiers, bottles, and breast pump parts with a bottle brush.

You can also use a bottle brush to clean pacifiers, bottles, and parts of a breast pump. This will save you money on non-compostable throwaway brushes and rags.

The best part is that you don't even have to buy one. Most of us already have these in our kitchens (at least I do), so why not use them?

Plastic containers are great for saving food and keeping it fresh, but if you have a lot of them, they can become an expensive waste problem. Instead of putting away those old plastic containers, reuse them!

- Store dry foods (rice, pasta, etc.)
- Personal items (like shampoo bottles)
- If the water bottles are clean,
- Recycle as much as possible!

Recycling is the easiest way to reduce waste and save money. Recycling glass bottles, aluminum cans, paper, and plastic containers will not only help you get rid of trash, but it will also save you money on your utility bills. If you have enough room in your home or yard for a compost bin, use it to turn food scraps into fertilizer for your garden. Instead of buying expensive cleaning products from the store, try making your own with vinegar or lemon juice.

If you have a lot of old clothes, consider donating them to a charity. Some charities will come pick up the items from your house, while others ask that you drop them off at their location. This is a good way to reduce waste because it gives clothes to people who need them while keeping things out of landfills and making your home less cluttered.

We hope this chapter has shown you how easy it is to reduce waste and save money. Even if you can't afford to buy everything new, there are still plenty of ways for you to reduce your impact on the environment. By making small changes in your daily life and even using things that you might otherwise throw away, you can help keep our planet healthy.

Book 9: Off Grid Solar Power System How to Generate Energy

Solar power systems efficiently create energy without the utility company. Solar panels on your roof or in a field transform sunlight into energy for appliances and lights. The inverter distinguishes off-grid solar power systems. Unlike a stand-alone system, a hybrid system contains both solar panels and utility connections.

Off-grid solar power system

Off-grid solar power systems dominate green energy. They produce power from the sun and store it in batteries or other devices for usage at night. These systems are perfect for off-grid residences and companies who desire to use green energy.

How does off-grid solar electricity work?

Off-grid solar power systems may power homes and businesses. It stores solar energy in batteries for usage when required. Off-grid solar power systems have:

Solar panels absorb sunlight.

Inverter - turns DC (direct current) into AC (alternating current) for home appliances like lights, computers, TVs, and refrigerators; converts surplus DC back into AC after charging batteries to use later.

Off-grid solar power helps whom?

- You want to lower your carbon impact and be more sustainable.
- You utilize a well and septic system since you don't have municipal water or sewer.
- You're sick of high utility costs but don't want to give up hot water heaters and freezers.

Off-grid solar electricity has what advantages?

Energy bill reduction is a growing trend. It'll grow worse when fossil fuel prices rise. What if you could get the advantages of off-grid living without changing your lifestyle? Off-grid solar power provides clean energy and utility bill savings!

Off-grid solar power system installation cost?

Installing an off-grid solar power system costs depends on many aspects. Consider your home's size and electricity use first. The second decision is whether to buy or outsource a system.

Your home's size determines how many panels each room needs to be powered by one panel. For instance, four rooms with two panels each would need eight panels (4 x 2). This means we should establish what sort of setup works best within our budget before purchasing any equipment because prices vary based on brand and other considerations like shipping costs or installation expenses if hiring someone else!

- Off-grid solar power systems create energy without cables.
- If there is adequate sunshine, this technique may be used everywhere. You'll have clean electricity from your solar panels even if power cables are down or damaged.
- Stand-alone or hybrid off-grid systems exist.
- Unlike a hybrid system, a stand-alone system never links to the grid.
- Stand-alone systems are good for distant regions without an electrical grid, but they frequently need backup generators for power outages or overcast days when sunlight isn't enough.

Hybrid solar power systems employ both off-grid and on-grid energy depending on availability. This system is more costly than an all-inclusive off-grid solution, but it allows you to connect certain items directly to solar energy while others, like refrigerators, use standard electricity.

Stand-alone systems are independent of utility providers and the electrical grid. They can power isolated cottages or dwellings without power cables.

These systems' major parts:

- Energy-generating solar panels
- Inverter (DC-to-AC)
- Solar-powered batteries
- Hybrid panels generate power.

Hybrid solar panels generate energy during the day and store it in batteries for nighttime or overcast days. If you want to live off-grid but can't afford enough solar panels to power your house, this is a good solution. Hybrid systems may be utilized with grid-connected equipment to protect against storm disruptions.

Hybrid systems use solar panels and utilities.

The grid-tied PV system generates solar power for your home's electric meter. If you require more electricity than your solar panels create, the grid will provide it instead of fossil fuels.

Solar power systems are an excellent alternative to utility companies. They're a great alternative to nuclear and conventional fuels.

- Solar power is an eco-friendly option for residential and commercial electricity.
- Off-Grid Solar Power System Benefits
- It powers homes, offices, and businesses.
- It can power equipment in distant places without a power infrastructure.

Off-Grid Solar Power System Drawbacks

Off-grid solar has drawbacks. Because you must purchase all the equipment and pay for installation, grid-connected ones are cheaper. If your home or business is not connected to the electricity grid, your excess solar panel electricity cannot be sold back into the grid or used by nearby residents who do not have renewable energy systems (unless they pay a premium).

The inverter distinguishes off-grid solar power systems. Solar panels turn sunshine into residential power. However, if solar panels are off-grid, their extra energy must be discarded.

You need to store this extra energy to use when there isn't enough sunlight for your panels or when it's nighttime and no one is using electricity.

Power storage is essential.

Power storage is required. This stores daytime energy and utilizes it when there's no sun. Batteries, which store electricity and can be recharged, work best.

Solar system types

Grid-tied and off-grid solar systems exist.

A grid-tied system, which connects to your home's electrical panel and sends electricity into the grid, is the most prevalent. These store energy in batteries. If you want one, read our chapter on "How to Make Your Home Run on Solar Energy."

If you want something simpler, more portable, or can't live far from an electrical grid, an off-grid solution may be appropriate for you! This configuration generates all your power from DC solar panels. Amazon has several gadgets with built-in converters that convert DC energy into AC for appliances like lights and refrigerators!

Selecting solar panels

Choosing solar panels might be difficult for beginners. It might be hard to choose among so many possibilities. We'll discuss the best techniques to select a solar panel in this part.

How much power do you need first? No matter how large your system is, low-voltage appliances (anything that plugs straight into an outlet) won't require much energy. However, microwaves and stoves require more electricity than lower voltage gadgets, thus enough solar panels may be needed.

Installation locations

Off-grid solar power systems work best in sunny locations. If you live in a shady area or want to install your system on an east-facing roof (where it's shaded by morning), consider a pole-mounted tracker.

For example, if you live in California and want to install 4 kW of panels—a popular size for residential systems—near Los Angeles or San Diego, where there are lots of bright days and mild nights (which makes them simpler to cool).

PV panel

The most crucial portion of any off-grid system is a solar photovoltaic panel, which powers everything else. Monocrystalline, polycrystalline, and amorphous (thin film) panels are available.

Monocrystalline panels, composed of single crystals sliced into wafers, cost more than polycrystalline or amorphous but provide more energy per square foot. Polycrystalline cells are cheaper but less effective than monocrystalline and heavier since they have numerous parts fused into one block instead of one slice. Amorphous solar cells cost even less than polycrystalline but are less efficient at converting sunlight into electricity. They're used on small devices like calculators and watches because their small surface area makes them less likely to break during transportation to construction sites where installing them may require working outdoors in harsh conditions like high winds or extreme heat/cold temperatures (which could cause cracks).

Solar power systems need charge controllers. Charge controllers safeguard batteries from overcharging, which shortens their lifetime. They also let you control power draw to charge the battery securely and effectively.

PWM or MPPT charge controllers are available. PWM controllers are cheaper but require more maintenance than MPPTs because they wear out faster under heavy use conditions like those found on RVs or boats, where there may be frequent starts/stops during travel periods and frequent changes in sun exposure caused by changing locations throughout each day's journey across land/water surfaces alike. MPPTs last longer because they don't have any moving parts.

Solar electricity is an excellent alternative to utility power. It doesn't emit pollutants or toxic byproducts like other power production methods, making it environmentally friendly. Talk to an expert about installing an off-grid solar system in your house or company!

Book 10: A Survival Guide

You've undoubtedly contemplated life without the grid. Have you imagined it? How would you remain warm and safe? Imagine living off the earth. This guide will explain everything. Read on!

Filtering water

Water filtration is the most crucial and difficult component of existence. Many water filters and purifying systems have benefits and downsides.

- Water filters: These devices filter water using a membrane with small holes. This lets you drink from your source without worrying about getting sick—if your filter works! Before consuming water from a gravity-fed device like an emergency backpacker's water bottle, be sure it includes a filter cartridge or use another way to remove microorganisms.
- Water purifiers: If you know the toxins in your supply, they may be useful, but some need energy or other resources that may not be accessible during an emergency.
- Bottles with straws: Users may reach both sides of these bottles without pumps or tubes, making them less probable.
- Bottles with tubes: Users may reach both sides without pumps or tubes, making them less probable than other varieties.
- Only straws: This approach is preferred since it doesn't need any extra equipment.

Getting Firewood

Don't chop trees. Find dead branches or twigs for fuel.

Don't burn rubbish or combustible stuff. These can easily start a fire that will spread to your campsite and damage the land around it, making it harder for others to enjoy their time outdoors and putting you at risk of burns or smoke inhalation if there are strong winds blowing through your campsite at night when it's cold outside in winter (or summer, depending on where you live in North America).

If possible, avoid gasoline since it has a history of being dangerous when used improperly, such as spilling some onto clothing while refueling cars/trucks, which causes them to wear said outfit while doing other tasks involving machinery and sharp objects like axes, which creates an explosive situation where people could die instantly due to injuries sustained while trying to get

- Shelter construction
- Safely locate.
- Shelter from nature.
- Build a shelter with adequate good-quality materials.
- Make the shelter weatherproof and warm for living.
- Fishing, hunting

Hunting and fishing may provide sustenance in the wild. To capture local animals, you must know their habits. Set traps for rabbits or squirrels, make snares for birds, dig holes or utilize deadfalls (branched trees) for raccoons, opossums, and other small animals. use baited hooks on long lines above fish-feeding water; spear fish through their eyes at night when sleeping in shallow waters like ponds or lakes, but only after learning which species are safe to eat!

If it's too chilly outdoors in winter, you need to know how to construct a rain shelter to avoid pneumonia while living without power!

Solar water purification.

Solar stills cleanse water well. It's simple to create using the ingredients. You'll need:

- Several quarts of water in a bucket or pail.
- soil or sand scooped from the earth that's loose and porous (you may use soil from around your home, but make sure it's chemical-free)
- A translucent plastic sheeting (tarp) to cover your container
- Steps to live off the grid
- The grid provides energy, water, and other services to your house. Off-grid people don't have these.

Find out whether you may legally be disconnected from all local utilities and follow the steps.

In case of emergencies like storms or floods that cut off access to grocery shops and farmers markets, save enough food and supplies for at least three months, the duration of winter till spring.

Know your global location.

Locate yourself first. Avoid getting lost and assist others find their way home. Use landmarks like mountains or rivers to find your location without a GPS signal or map.

Know how to obtain assistance. If possible, call 911 from your cell phone or radio for emergency services, including police and firefighters who can help with medical emergencies like broken bones or burns from lightning strikes near trees during storms (this happens often).

Prepare to survive.

Wild survival requires preparation. Know what you're doing to prepare. You must know how to gather water and food, remain warm and dry, traverse the wilderness, defend oneself from predators (human and animal), manage injuries and sickness, and accomplish all of this while carrying just what you can carry on your back.

If any of these are new to you, read up before going into nature alone with just your wits and instincts!

- Electricity
- Make a battery first. Battery storage is the most efficient and versatile. You'll need:
- A working vehicle battery or other lead-acid battery
- Metal and wire cutters

Following those steps: 1) Cut two pieces of metal, two shorter than the other four, approximately one inch long. 2) Use a wire stripper to remove insulation from one wire's ends. 3) Bend each piece's end. 4) Twist them together to join them. 5). Place this new device in a water-filled container. 6). Charge it! It's simple!

Make fire.

Survival requires fire. It can cook, light, filter water, and signal for aid.

Knowing how to build fire may be one of the most vital skills to acquire if you're in a scenario without power or a grid. People have invented several methods to ignite fires without matches or lighters (which may not work if your batteries die). Each approach has fundamental steps:

Need water.
Survival requires water. It's vital. Before you need water, you should know how to get there securely. In metropolitan areas, knowing where your fire hydrant or water main is may be enough (albeit they may not operate if no one has maintained them since the grid went down). Finding a stream or lake in nature is exciting since it takes work!

In addition to knowing where your water will come from during an emergency like this one, I also recommend stockpiling several gallons at home so that if we lose access again, there's still enough for everyone until their next paycheck comes through so they can buy more bottles/bags/etc.

Food is vital.
- It maintains your body and mind. Starvation will kill you.
- Food comes from towns and the wild. Food may be purchased or bartered in towns or in the wild.
- Calories aren't equal! To be healthy, you need a range of vitamins and minerals from diverse sources, and certain calories keep hunger at bay longer than others!

Warmth and dryness need shelter.
Shelter keeps you warm and dry. You may use sticks and leaves to make a shelter without a tent or tarp. If you have a blanket or sleeping bag, you may put it on the ground and cover yourself with it at night or in bad weather.

Wilderness travel
If you're unfamiliar with your surroundings, navigating the wilderness is challenging. Here are some ways to reorient yourself when things go wrong:

Locate yourself. Before going on an excursion, know as much as you can about your place. This includes learning about your destination's geology, climate, and flora and fauna. It also entails studying how distant from society it is so that if anything occurs while out there, aid will arrive swiftly before anybody gets wounded by exposure, malnutrition, dehydration, etc.

Return home! Always carry a survival kit with water purification tablets or chlorine dioxide tablets to make contaminated water drinkable, medical supplies like bandages, food rations like energy bars or dried fruit packets, matches/lighters, etc. Always carry these little items—they might save your life in an emergency!

Survival Kits provide equipment and materials for wilderness survival. If you are lost or wounded while outdoors, you'll need a survival pack to return home safely.

The kit should fit in your backpack or pocket yet be large enough for all the essentials: water purification pills; bandages; painkillers (ibuprofen); lighter/matches; flashlight/batteries; rope/zip ties (for constructing shelters); cordage material like fishing line or paracord bracelet—anything else that could be useful in an emergency!

Keep Safe

Protect yourself. It's crucial to know how to defend oneself from all of the wild's dangers.

The Elements Climate will determine where and how long you put up your base camp. Consider your region's weather and dress properly (with backup plans). Avoid storms and harsh heat/cold to reduce stress and stay safe!

Animals: There are many creatures on Earth that may wish to eat us! Put traps around old campsites and protect food remnants so other animals don't get into them.

I hope this chapter helped you survive in the wild, and good luck on your next expedition. Always be prepared, so you can handle any scenario!

Book 11: Defense System in Your Home

You've probably heard about how the power grid can fail in the news. But how does that affect you? How do you get ready? If the grid goes down and stays down for a long time, what will happen? You may not have given these questions much thought before, but now is the time to start. When the grid goes down, you have to find other ways to power your home. Make sure you have a backup engine or another way to power your home. You can get solar panels for your home and even solar turbines that connect to your solar panels. There are also wind generators and hand-crank engines with spinning wheels that can be used to charge batteries.

The power grid could break down.

The power grid could break down. You can attack the power grid. A natural accident or even a computer attack that affects the whole country at once could take down the power grid.

The best way to protect yourself from these situations is to have a defense system in your home that will keep you safe when things go wrong and help you stay alive long enough to get back on track when the dust settles (or doesn't).

- When the grid goes down, you have to find other ways to power your home.
- When the grid goes down, there are a few things you can do to make sure your home is safe and secure.
- Keeping thieves out of your house: If someone breaks into your house, they will be looking for food, water, and a place to stay. They may try to take these things from you. To keep them from coming into your house to begin with:
- Put deadbolts on all the doors that lead outside (or, if possible, inside as well).
- Set up security cams in key spots around the property, near power sources, so they can keep running even when there is no electricity.
- Install motion monitors near windows and doors that will sound a warning if someone opens them while everyone is sleeping inside.

Make sure you have a generator as a back-up.

If you have a generator, it's best to keep it always charged and ready to go. This will make sure your home has power even if the grid goes down.

Generators can be expensive, but they are worth it if you want to be able to take care of your family in a case when there is no power from the grid or public services company. You might also want to think about using solar panels or wind machines to make energy so you don't have to rely on engines that run on fuel alone.

If you can, try not to use any electronics in your house for a few days after an EMP attack. This will help keep your electronics from being damaged by electromagnetic interference (EMI).

Wind machines

Wind generators are a good way to get power away from the grid. They are easy to set up and keep up, not too expensive, and can charge batteries and make power. Off-grid power can also come from engines that you turn by hand. These gadgets use spinning wheels to make power that can be used in situations or when the grid goes down (like when you get snowed in).

You can also save batteries and charge them.

You can also save batteries and charge them with the sun or other forms of energy when you can. This is a great way to charge your battery bank if you have a windmill.

Batteries are important because they keep your phone charged and they keep things like lights and radios working when the power goes out. Use your solar panels if you have them set up at home. You might need more power than normal because of all the extra people who will be coming over after dark.

A back-up plans

- It's important to have a back-up method in case the power goes out or something bad happens. A backup system can be as easy as an engine and battery or as complicated as a solar panel grid with batteries.
- Power blackouts can happen at any time, even when you don't expect them.
- They can be caused by storms, earthquakes, or hurricanes, among other things.

- They can also happen when someone accidentally flips the wrong switch or when mistakes happen with power lines or transformers, like when too much electricity flows through them at once, like during a lightning storm.

System for safety

A security system is an important part of your home that protects you from burglars and other dangerous people or things. It's a set of devices that keep an eye on the safety of your home and let you know if someone breaks in or if there's a fire or smoke using a different device, like an alarm clock or a smartphone app.

Security systems can be used to find people who are on your land without permission and let you know right away. Some systems also let you talk to them through a speaker system so that they don't run away before the cops come.

Cameras for security

The best way to keep an eye on your home when you're not there is with security cams. Both wired and cordless versions have their pros and cons. Wiring your security camera means running lines through the walls and ceilings of your house. If you don't know what you're doing, this can be hard, especially if you live in an older home with brick walls instead of drywall.

Wireless cameras are easier to set up, but they need a good internet link to work properly (the information from the camera needs to go somewhere else). If you get a wired system, all those wires will be hidden behind the walls where no one can see them. This makes it look better when people come over because everything is neat and clean and no wires are out in the open for everyone to see.

Movement detectors

Motion monitors are used to tell when something is moving in a room or area. They can be used to find animals, people, and cars that are moving. Motion monitors are often used as an alarm system in homes and businesses because they let you know if someone sneaks onto your property.

- Remote Surveillance Cameras
- Movement detectors
- Solar Panels
- Wind turbine (to move water and clean it)
- Generator

Generators are an important part of the backup power source for every home. If you live in an area where the power goes out often, you can use a generator to power your home when the power is out.

Generators come in many shapes and sizes and can be driven by gasoline, diesel, or natural gas. Portable generators are light enough that you can move them from one place to another if you need to. Stationary generators, on the other hand, are forever placed on your land.

Water Pump and Filter

The water pump and filter are important to your life when you are off the grid. Without them, you won't be able to get clean water to drink, and if you drink something that isn't clean, you could get sick. A reverse osmosis system is a good option because it will get rid of germs and other harmful things in the water supply, making it safe to drink.

Another important part of this system is that it purifies the water. This way, you can make sure that all germs are gone from your drinking water before you or anyone else in your home drinks it.

You can power your home even if you're not connected to the grid.

The fridge and freezer are two of the most important home tools. They keep food cold, so it won't go bad as fast and you can eat it whenever you want. But this doesn't matter if you don't have power because your food will thaw in a few days or even hours.

Use a sealed box with ice packs or other cooling materials inside to store food without having to freeze it. This will keep everything cool for a long time (up to several weeks). You can do this with any kind of container that has a good enough seal to keep out wetness from the outside air: If the Tupperware containers are big enough, they work well. Rubbermaid boxes are also great because their lids are already connected. No matter what kind of containers you choose, make sure they won't leak.

The normal home needs a backup power source for times when the weather is bad or when something unexpected happens. When it comes to the safety of your home, you should be ready for anything, but how?

The first thing you should do is make sure every room in your house has a smoke alarm. So, if there is ever an electrical fire or other emergency, they will go off and let everyone in the house know right away so they can get out safely. If there aren't any smoke alarms yet, you should get them as soon as possible. The next step is to make sure that each room has its own light source, like a lamp, so that if one bulb breaks, it won't affect them all at once, like it could with overhead lights, which could make several rooms dark at the same time without anyone noticing until later, when they realize something is wrong.

Food can be kept in the freezer

You can put food in the freezer, but if you don't have power, the food will melt in a few days or even hours. If you don't have power to cook with gas and rely on solar or battery-powered stoves as a backup, this may not be a choice for you. Cell phones won't charge either if they aren't plugged into the grid.

Your home's security system is an important part of it

If you want to build a house, a security system is an important part of it that protects you from burglars and other dangerous things. Installing the right security system in your home is important to keep you safe from all sorts of dangers, like burglaries and fires.

There are many different kinds of these systems on the market today, but you should always choose ones that are reliable, cost-effective, and easy to install. You should also make sure to keep them in good shape so they work well all the time.

The security of a well-prepared home is made up of many layers.

A home that is well-prepared has multiple layers of security that keep out burglars, natural disasters, and other dangers. In this section, we'll talk about the most important parts of a home power system that is safe and will last for a long time.

System for security: While you are away, a good safety system will keep thieves and wild animals away. It should be able to detect movement inside or outside your home and send you a text message or email so you can take action (like turning off the lights).

Wind Turbine: This device gets energy from the wind by having blades placed on an axis and linked directly below them by gears that spin when strong winds blowing at speeds of more than 20 mph (32 km/h) pass directly over them. This rotation makes electricity, which is sent through lines that are hidden underground until they reach storage areas, where extra energy is kept until it is needed later.

So, that's the end of it. This chapter should have given you some ideas for your own home defense system. Feel free to get in touch with us at any time if you need more information or help with your project.

Book 12: Medical And First Aid Survival

When the power goes out, it's important to know how to take care of yourself! When you can't get medical help, you'll need your own first aid kit. You will need to check all of the medicines you have at home or at work, including those you buy over-the-counter, those you get from a doctor, and insulin. Make sure you have enough of everything you need for a full week or a month, based on how long you think it will be before the utilities are back on. If you don't have electricity, your lighting might not work either. Buy strong flashlights with LED bulbs and, if possible, make sure they are waterproof. Also, buy lanterns with glow sticks built in so you can turn them on when you need to without having to shake them for hours until they light up.

Bandages

Bandages stop bleeding and keep cuts from getting worse. You can use cotton, paper, or plastic to make them. If you don't have any bandages with you when you need to give first aid, it's best to make do with torn-up pieces of cloth or clothes.

Pain killers

Painkillers can help with headaches, aches in the muscles, and toothaches. They can also be used to treat sore lips and back pain.

Painkillers should be used with care because they can have side effects like making you feel dizzy, sick, or sleepy.

Cleaning the Water

You can use a water filter or boil your water for at least 10 minutes to make it safe to drink.

The best way to make sure that water is clean is to boil it for at least 10 minutes. But if you are in an emergency or don't have a stove or fire pit, this can take a long time and isn't very useful. In these cases, it might be better to use iodine pills because they only need 30 seconds of touch time with the water before they are safe to drink. Iodine is also less likely than chlorine (bleach) to cause damaging side effects like skin itching when used wrong, but it should still be treated with care if it is eaten over and over for a long time.

Alcohol Swabs (or hand sanitizer)

Alcohol swabs are a great way to clean and disinfect cuts and scrapes. You can also use them to clean your hands, but if you have hand sanitizer in your first aid kit, you can use that instead.

Alcohol is a sanitizer that kills bacteria and viruses on the skin. This makes it a great way to kill germs before they get into your body through cuts or scrapes.

When you put an alcohol swab on a cut or scrape:

Cleanse the area around the wound with light pressure to get rid of dirt and other waste. Then, dry it completely with a clean cloth or paper towel to stop it from bleeding.

If there is pus in your wound, put pressure on it until it stops dripping out. Then, if you want, you can apply an antibiotic ointment like Neosporin. This will help prevent infection and speed up cell regeneration in damaged tissue cells, which will help the wound heal faster.

Insect Repellent

Insect protection is an important part of a first-aid kit. Insect bites can cause infections, so it's important to have a good insect repellant on hand to avoid bites and their possible effects.

In many parts of the world, insects like mosquitoes and ticks are common, so it's best to avoid getting bitten at all times of the year, not just in the summer when these pests seem to be more common.

Pain Relief

The most important thing to do if you get burned is to get away from the source of heat as soon as you can. Next, put a cream or gel on the burn to ease the pain and swelling. You can do this by rubbing it gently into your skin with clean fingers or a clean cloth.

If you don't have access to these things, you can try the following:

Aloe Vera Gel: Cut off the bottom of an aloe leaf and rub it directly on burns or sunburns until the gel is absorbed by the skin. Never use ice or ice water on a burn.

- Water and Epsom Salt: Mix equal parts of water and Epsom salts until they make a paste that you can't use, then spread it all over the affected area.
- Butterfly bandages are also called butterfly closure strips.
- Butterfly Closure Strips, also called butterfly patches, are medical strips that stick to wounds and close them. You can use them on your fingers, toes, and other body parts because they come in different sizes and shapes.
- Butterfly Closure Strips are also made of rubber or something else that isn't latex, and they are also clean.

First-Aid Kit for Yourself

You have a book on first aid, but just reading it and hoping you remember everything isn't enough. You should also have a first-aid kit with everything you might need in an emergency.

- Bandages
- Gauze pads (different sizes)
- This is useful for keeping patches in place on cuts that are bleeding heavily or might need to be glued shut later if they are too deep to sew up yourself without the right tools or training.
- Makeshift Splints
- A splint is a great way to keep a broken bone or joint from moving. You can make them out of almost anything you have on hand, but here are some of the most common:
- Wood
- Metal (e.g., a car jack)
- Plastic, such as PVC pipe or cardboard,

CPR

CPR is the best way to give first aid to someone who isn't breathing. If you need to give CPR to someone, here are some simple steps:

See if they are breathing. If someone isn't breathing, you should start chest compressions.

Put your hands on either side of their chest, with your fingers pointing toward their armpits (the center of gravity). Position yourself so that both of your shoulders are in line with theirs. This will help prevent back injuries and make compression more effective by spreading the weight evenly across both sides of the body instead of just pressing down with one hand at a time, which is how most people would do it if they didn't have someone like me there to show them what to do.

Try pushing down about 2 inches, but only as hard as you need to so you don't hurt internal organs or break ribs or bones. Then let go fully and do it again until help comes (or until you die).

How to Treat Shock

In shock, the parts of the body don't get enough blood or air. This can happen if the person is hurt, thirsty, or is bleeding. Shock can kill you if it isn't handled right away, so you need to see a doctor right away.

If you've been hurt and are showing signs of shock, like weakness, confusion, or cold skin, do the following:

If you can, lay down with your feet raised above your head.

If you can, raise your legs higher than your head.

If you don't have access to emergency equipment, use a tourniquet before putting on pressure patches.

Making A Diagnosis

The first step in healing any sickness or accident is to figure out what's wrong. If you don't know what's wrong with your patient, you can't figure out how to help them.

Let's start by looking at some of the most common signs and symptoms of different sicknesses and accidents. Once you know what kind of accident or illness they have, you can decide if they need to be taken to the hospital right away.

If your patient isn't having serious symptoms like shortness of breath or chest pain, you may not need to worry just yet. However, if you have any doubts about their condition, even if everything seems fine, you should get them to a doctor as soon as possible before trying anything else, like the self-treatment methods described below this section in another chapter called "How to Treat Yourself in an Emergency."

Know what to do in case of an emergency.

- Know what's around you.
- Make sure you know how to read a map and use a guide before you need them to save your life.
- Learn how to read topographic maps and how to use GPS devices. If you don't have these tools, you can also learn how to use the sun and stars to find your way.

First, you need to know the basics.

- Splinting: You will need to know how to make a splint for any broken bones or sprains you find on your journey, whether they are in a limb or in the body as a whole.
- Controlling bleeding: You'll want to know how fast someone can die from bleeding, especially if they're already in shock from losing blood when they're hurt (which they probably will be). This means knowing how long it takes for an average person's body weight in liters of blood to be lost before they go into hypovolemic shock (1 L = 5 oz). Then, you should find out what kinds of materials are available in nature where you live so that if someone gets hurt outside and there aren't any hospitals nearby (like, say, after World War III), you can have something useful like gauze pads ready to use instead.
- Don't get scared because you think your cuts will kill you.
- Remember that you can live with a wound, even if it looks bad and seems like it should kill you.

Don't freak out and think, "I'm going to die from my wounds." This will only make things worse, especially if you are far from help. When you've been hurt, you need to stay calm and try not to freak out. If you do, your body will go into shock, which could kill you or cause other problems when you go to the hospital for treatment.

If you can, don't ignore wounds because they get worse over time. This means that even small cuts or scrapes can get sick if left unchecked for long enough, so keep an eye on how they're doing (but don't look at them directly) as often as you can. If something looks really bad, you should get professional help as soon as possible. Leaving serious injuries untreated for more than 24 hours could cause permanent damage or even amputations due to bacteria growth. This could happen if you don't get the right care from trained professionals who know what to do before you try anything else, like using home remedies like rubbing alcohol, which might seem like a good idea but usually end up doing more harm than good.

Use a dressing to stop cuts from bleeding and keep them clean.

The best patch is one that is clean and sterile, but you can also use cloth or cotton bandages. Make sure the bandage is tight enough to stop the bleeding, but not so tight that it hurts or cuts off the blood flow. If you can, put an antibiotic cream on the wound before you wrap it in bandages or strips of fabric (like T-shirts). Change your bandages at least once a day until they are no longer needed. This will depend on how bad your injury is and how fast it heals, but don't wait too long! If you can, wash your hands before touching any part of someone else's body, including your own. This is because germs could spread if two people who aren't healthy enough for this yet touch each other.

Keep some sort of first aid kit with you at all times.

- This is especially important if you don't have access to medical care or live in a remote place.
- What you put in your first aid kit will rely on what kinds of accidents are widespread in your area and what kinds of materials are available nearby, but here's a general list:
- Bandages of different sizes
- Wipes with antiseptics and wipes with alcohol (to clean cuts)
- Pain relievers like aspirin or ibuprofen (this can be important if someone has broken bones or other major injuries).
- Antibiotic cream for wounds that aren't healing well or have infections.

Learn the basics of sewing so you can fix clothes or cuts.

With time and practice, you can learn how to sew. The first thing you should know is how to sew on a button, which involves using your hands and eyes to guide the needle through the fabric. To do this, put your thumb on top of one side of the button, put two fingers under it, and push down while you sew.

Use heavy-duty thread or even dental floss, which won't come apart, to make sure your stitches are strong enough. If there are any extra ends sticking out after stitching up an injury or fixing a piece of clothing, cut them off with scissors or clippers before putting another layer of material over them so they don't poke out later!

Even if you are not a doctor or nurse, you should learn CPR.
Heart-lung resuscitation is what CPR stands for. It is a way to help someone who isn't breathing or has no pulse. Chest compressions and mouth-to-mouth breathing are used. If you want to be ready for a case in which someone needs medical help right away, you should learn how to do CPR.

If you find someone who isn't breathing and doesn't have a pulse, the first thing you should do is call 911 (or whatever service is similar in your area). Next:

If you can't, skip ahead to the next steps. Do 30 chest compressions at a rate of 100 per minute. This means that each compression should take 2 seconds. This means that every time you press down on their chest, you should count "one thousand one" and then let go before pressing again. Keep doing this until help comes.

- If you know how to help yourself, you have a better chance of getting through a crisis.
- Learn how to start and keep a fire going. You'll need fire to stay warm, cook food, clean water, and send out signals for help.
- Know how to treat cuts and accidents properly so they don't get sick or get worse over time because of bad care. This includes using a wound wrap. The best way is to keep dirt out of them at all times. If there isn't any clean water, try using soap instead. Soap has antiseptic properties that can help keep you from getting an infection after being cut by something sharp, like a piece of glass or metal from an explosion nearby that sent debris flying everywhere and hurt many people, including themselves.

Trauma

A trauma kit is a group of medical items used to treat wounds. You can make your own or buy one, but both should have the following:

Four-by-four-inch sterile paper pads

Wraps and bandages made of elastic that come in different sizes: 1 inch wide for fingers, 2 inches wide for wrists, ankles, and upper arms, and 4 inches wide for legs, bodies, or even bigger.

- The tape is 1 inch thick.
- Shears and tweezers
- Cream or gel for burns

You might also want to add things like wound cleaner, hydrogen peroxide solution, and antibiotic cream. If you don't have any clean water on hand when you need to treat an injury, you could use rubbing alcohol instead to clean the wound before applying other treatments like creams or gels.

- To get ready for a long-term survival situation, here are some more things to get.
- Tablets that clean water
- Filter for portable water
- Tarpaulin (to catch rain, make a cover, etc.)
- Duct tape can be used to fix things and do other things.
- Compass (for finding your way)
- call mirror (to call for help)
- When the power goes out and you can't get medical help, you'll need your own first aid kit.
- A first-aid kit should be in your home, office, and car. A good kit will have the following:
- Bandages of different sizes
- Gauze pads
- Medical tape
- Scissors
- Sterile gloves

Wipes or liquid antiseptics like Betadine that kill germs

You will need to check all of the medicines you have at home or at work, including those you buy over-the-counter, those you get from a doctor, and insulin.

If you are taking any of the following, you may need extra supplies:

- Antibiotics (for example penicillin)
- Medications for high blood pressure, such as diuretics,
- Medication for diabetes

The best way to get ready for a power outage is to buy enough goods to last a week or a month. This will help you make sure you have enough food, drink, medicine, and other necessities. If the power goes out and your refrigerator stops working (or if you don't have one), make sure there are no fresh things inside that could go bad over time. Also, make sure the batteries in all of your flashlights are good so they don't die when you're trying to find something in the dark!

You should also think about stocking up on first aid items like bandages, gauze pads, and antibiotic ointment, as well as tools like scissors or knives if you can, to help treat any injuries that might happen in an emergency situation like this one, where hospitals and clinics might not be open due to their own problems...

If you don't have electricity, your lighting might not work either.
Your flashlight can help you find your way in the dark and save your life. If you don't have electricity, your lighting might not work either. You'll need something else to help you see in the dark.

If you don't have electricity, your lighting might not work either. You will need another way to see in the dark. Candles, oil lamps, or battery-powered lanterns with LED lights will give off enough light for basic tasks like reading and cooking, but they won't give off enough light for navigating unfamiliar places or signaling for help at night if you get lost outside after an emergency (like an earthquake).

- Buy strong flashlights with LED bulbs and, if possible, make sure they are waterproof.
- LEDs are more efficient and last longer

- They're brighter than incandescent lights, so you'll be able to see better in the dark.
- They are also more sturdy than light bulbs, so if you drop them or hit them against rocks while hiking in the woods (which you probably will), they won't break as easily.
- LED lights use less energy than other types of lighting, so if you use batteries instead of solar panels or wind turbines to power your devices, they won't drain your battery as fast.
- LEDs are good for the environment because they don't contain mercury like some light bulbs do. Since there's no glass covering on top, there's also less chance that any stray drops will break into pieces in your backpack later.
- Buy lights with LED bulbs. They use less energy, last longer, and give off more light than regular electric bulbs.

If you can choose between a hand-crank flashlight and a portable battery-powered one, choose the hand-crank one because it will work even if there is no electricity (like in an emergency). It also gives you a way to charge other devices that have USB ports, like cell phones or tablets. Just plug them straight into the spinning mechanism.

Don't shake glow sticks until they light up enough for you to see. Instead, keep shaking them until they reach full brightness within 5 seconds after being shaken hard several times over each other before turning off again, so you don't waste time trying to get out of the dark when there is no light source nearby.

When the power goes out, it's important to know how to take care of yourself!

Make sure you have a first aid kit and you know how to use it. You should also know how to handle simple wounds like cuts and burns. If someone in your group gets sick or hurt, they need to see a doctor right away before their condition gets worse.

Plan what to do if something goes wrong. If someone got hurt, what would happen? How are we going to take care of them until help comes? What if a wild animal bite someone? Have we got enough tools to help the patient?

Knowing these answers ahead of time will save time when everyone is worried about what happened and doing their best to not only stay alive but also heal from whatever happened, which could include psychic damage.

The most important thing to remember is that you'll have a better chance of getting through an emergency if you know how to take care of yourself. Even if you're not a doctor or nurse, you should always have some kind of first aid kit with you and learn CPR. Anyone who wants to be ready for anything needs to know about medicine and first aid.

CONCLUSION

In closing, the Bible has a lot to teach us about life, including how to stay alive in the desert. Even though the Bible doesn't talk about specific "no grid" survival projects, its lessons and ideas can still be used in current conditions. By reading and following the Bible's advice, people can gain information and skills that will help them handle difficult scenarios, such as those that might come up in a no-grid survival situation. In the end, the Bible can help you survive in any way, both physically and spiritually. Overall, "No Grid Survival Projects - The Bible" is a well-written and useful book for people who want to learn more about living off the grid.

BONUS:

VIDEO BONUS ON BEEKIPING

Growing Hydroponic Vegetable Garden at Home

VIDEO for Prepper's Water survival guide

Made in United States
Troutdale, OR
10/01/2023

13338493R00064